The Cowpens—
Guilford Courthouse
Campaign

GREAT BATTLES OF HISTORY

HANSON W. BALDWIN, *General Editor*

Also by BURKE DAVIS

THEY CALLED HIM STONEWALL

GRAY FOX: R. E. LEE AND THE CIVIL WAR

JEB STUART, THE LAST CAVALIER

TO APPOMATTOX

OUR INCREDIBLE CIVIL WAR

MARINE! THE LIFE OF GENERAL CHESTY PULLER

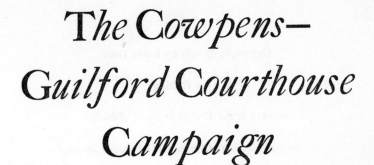

The Cowpens—Guilford Courthouse Campaign

BURKE DAVIS

J. B. LIPPINCOTT COMPANY

Philadelphia & New York

To Olivia Burwell and Irene Hester,
Librarians and friends

CONTENTS

MAPS

VIRGINIA.

Banister R.

TO RICHMOND
TO PETERSBURG
TO YORKTOWN

Dan R.

DIX'S FERRY

Yadkin R.

SALEM

GUILFORD COURTHOUSE

HILLSBORO

Haw R.

NORTH   CAROLINA

GILBERT TOWN
SALISBURY
RAMSOUR'S MILL

Little Pee Dee R.

Deep R.

SHERRILL'S FORD

CHARLOTTE

Catawba R.

CHEROKEE FORD
COWPENS

CHERAW

Cape Fear R.

Great Pee Dee R.

WINNSBOROUGH   CAMDEN

Broad R.

WILMINGTON

NINETY-SIX

Saluda R.

CAPE FEAR

SOUTH   CAROLINA

EUTAW SPRINGS

GEORGETOWN

N

MONKS CORNER

W   E

OCEAN

S

CHARLESTON

GEORGIA

ATLANTIC

The CAROLINAS
1780~1781

SCALE OF MILES

0   25   50

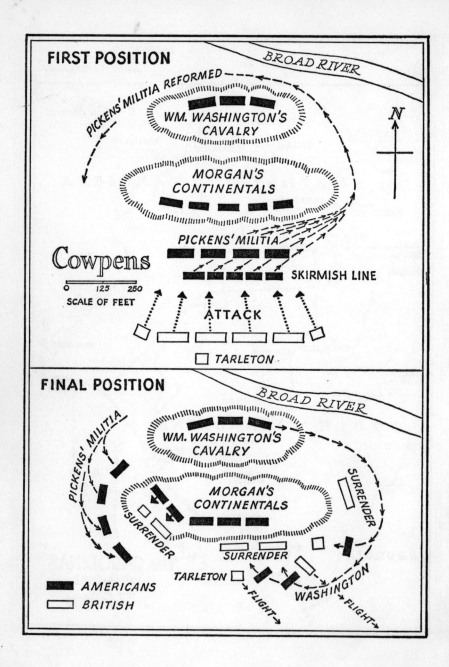

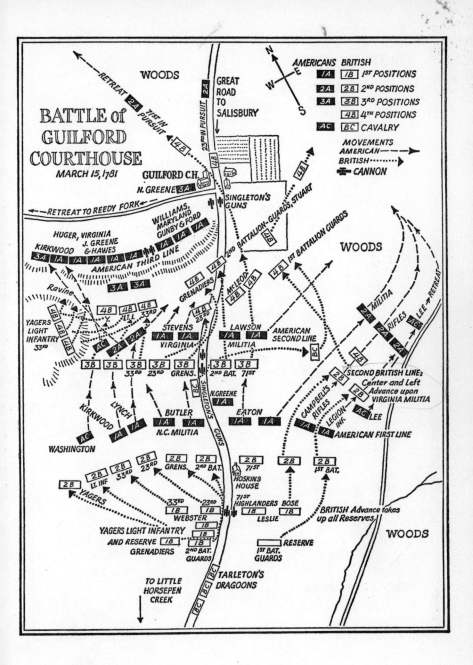

BATTLE of GUILFORD COURTHOUSE

MARCH 15, 1781

The Cowpens—
Guilford Courthouse
Campaign

Prelude

S THE DREARY YEAR 1780 DREW TO A close in the Carolina wilderness, the strange war of the American Revolution was almost six years old. The conflict opened by the daring Massachusetts farmers in '75 was to be settled in the little-known south —though in the December snows in the remote village of Charlotte, North Carolina, the prospect was beyond the imagination of anyone in the miserable little American army, including Maj. Gen. Nathanael Greene himself.

Veteran British military men had warned their political leaders. General Hervey, the Adjutant General, studied the maps of America when rebellion burst forth near Boston: The vast territory was thinly spread with about 3 million people. There were no cities, except for the few seaports. American fighting men had only to retreat into the wild hill country where no invader could safely follow. There were no inland strongholds to command the countryside, and except for the line of the Hudson River, no paths into the heart of the country.

The Americans might easily raise 150,000 troops. Even if Britain could spare 30,000 to 50,000 men, they must be carried over 3,000 miles of ocean. The prospect of anything beyond a naval war, with occupation of American ports and occasional raids, seemed madness to Hervey: "Taking America as it at present stands, it is impossible to conquer it with our British Army . . . to attempt to conquer it internally by our land force is as wild an idea as ever controverted commonsense."

But George III and his advisors had listened, instead, to colonial governors, who argued that thousands of loyal subjects would spring to arms against the rebels, and that the very sight of British regulars would end the uprising.

Thanks to this policy, Nathanael Greene was still alive, a veteran of the fierce fighting in the northern campaigns—now sent to kindle the faint flicker of hope in the south, where a new British campaign of invasion had been launched. It seemed almost too late.

War had seldom found two nations more poorly prepared. British military power had eroded in the years of peace under a succession of inept ministries. As late as December, 1774, the Navy's seamen had been reduced from 20,000 to 16,000, and the following year only 2,000 effectives were added. The militia was so poorly disciplined that it was thought unsafe to call it out. The King had insisted that the Army be bolstered by recruiting—but its 35,000 men were increased to only 55,000 in '75, and much time had been lost. There were also demands for troops in India, and on Gibraltar and Minorca.

George III turned to the German princes, and from

Hesse-Cassel, Hesse-Hanau, Brunswick, Waldeck, Anspach-Bayreuth, and Anhalt-Zerbst he contracted for 18,000 troops —the first of 30,000 German soldiers sent to America. Of these, 12,000 never returned (5,000 of the missing deserted to make a home in the new country).

The name "Hessians" was a misnomer for the variety of German troops, but more than half came from Hesse-Cassel, whose greedy ruler stripped his principality of one-fourth of its able-bodied men to collect English silver.

British manpower problems were never solved. At least one regiment of Highlanders mutinied at the docks when being shipped to America and fought other regulars sent to subdue them.

In America, things were even worse. Men had sprung to arms in the summer of '75, so that George Washington was able to besiege General Howe in Boston through the winter. But as cold weather came, desertions left the rebels but a handful of men. At one time there were only three rounds of ammunition for each American musket, and food was so scarce that there was a constant threat of mutiny. Troops thronged in and out of camp as they pleased; enlistments of almost all expired on Jan. 1, 1776.

Washington almost despaired: "Such a dearth of public spirit . . . I never saw before, and pray God's mercy I may never be witness to again . . . to enlist 500 men I am obliged to furlough 50 to a regiment. Such a mercenary spirit pervades the whole that I could not be surprised at any disaster. . . . Could I have foreseen what I have experienced and am likely to experience, no consideration on earth would have induced me to accept the command."

Yet, when spring came, "by hook or crook," as he said, Washington had rebuilt an army of almost 18,000, and with the aid of the captured big guns Gen. Henry Knox had dragged over the New England hills from Fort Ticonderoga, he drove the British from Boston. The war had fairly begun.

Howe went to sea and struck at New York in an enormous amphibious operation. More than 100 ships lay in the lower harbor as 25,000 British and Hessian troops were put ashore on Long Island; new ships came daily, as Lord Charles Cornwallis and Sir Henry Clinton arrived from the south. Washington's trenches had been well built, largely by Nathanael Greene, but his 18,000 were not enough, and the position on Long Island was a trap. Howe turned American lines in a fierce engagement at Brooklyn Heights, and rebel casualties were almost 2,000 men.

Washington had fatally divided his forces, leaving them open to attack by land and sea on a complex terrain—but with the aid of hundreds of Marblehead fishermen from Massachusetts in open boats, he moved the surviving troops into New York in darkness and fog. Washington and Greene would have burned the city, but were overruled by a council of war. There was another defeat at Kingsbridge, and then at Harlem Heights, and the British took New York, with sixty-seven guns and vast stores. A later fire destroyed part of the city, but it was to remain in British hands until the war was over.

Washington's retreat was up the River Bronx, where Howe followed, and fought him at White Plains, but won only a partial success, for the main British thrust was not delivered. A campaign had ended. There were no American victories, but here and there, regiments had fought so bravely as to wring respect from British veterans. As Lt. William Harcourt said: ". . . though [the Americans] seem to be ignorant of the precision, order, and even of the principles, by which large bodies are moved, yet they possess . . . activity and a spirit of enterprise. . . . Though it was once the fashion of this army to treat them in the most contemptible light, they are now become a formidable enemy."

Among the most dependable of Washington's troops in the fighting of 1776 were those of Delaware and Maryland, who had saved remnants of the fleeing army more than once. They were volunteers of the highest type, destined to hold together the American army until the end. Some of the finest of British regiments had also appeared—the 17th Light Dragoons, the 71st Highlanders, and the 33rd Foot.

A great many of the fresh British troops were by no means volunteers, but had been recruited by lies and liquor, or taken when drunk. Hundreds were vagrants from the London streets—but they were hardened, often desperate, men when they went into uniform, and made good soldiers.

In the early battles, the European style of close-order ranks under fire was forced upon the Americans by the British, and here the invaders excelled. Their uniforms, after the German pattern, were more ornamental than useful, with impractical scarlet coats and bright linings and facings, with high leather stocks to restrict movements of the head. The awkward hats did not shield the eyes from the sun. But even daily chores like washing white breeches, powdering hair, and cleaning brightwork improved British discipline, and made the redcoats more reliable in battle.

An English regiment had ten companies, eight for line duty, one of light infantry (for skirmishing and reconnaissance), and a crack company of grenadiers, equipped with grenades and launchers. The American organization had no such refinements, and regiments from the first varied widely in numbers. There were no regimental divisions into light infantry, grenadiers, and the like. Still, as the year ended, the Americans gave new proof of their mettle.

On a December night when the ice-choked Delaware River seemed impassable, Washington led his 3,000, "the wretched remains of a broken army," across the stream to fall upon sleeping Hessians at Trenton. In the past campaign, more than 5,000 American troops had been captured. Within a few days, without some victory to spur them on, most of Washington's remaining troops would go home at the end of their enlistments. With the aid of the Marblehead fishermen to ferry troops and guns, he accomplished a small miracle.

The army split into two columns and surprised the Germans, with one column led by Nathanael Greene; artillery broke up Hessian formations before they became effective, and the enemy force was destroyed, with 1,000 taken prisoner or wounded. Washington's casualties: four wounded. Washington then evaded chase by Charles Cornwallis and went into camp at Morristown, in the New Jersey hills, where desertions grew. Despite epidemics of smallpox and the departure of whole regiments, Washington survived the winter.

In March there was good news from New Hampshire—a French ship had brought 1,000 barrels of fine gunpowder, 11,000 musket flints, and many cases of arms and uniforms; many other French ships were reported on the way. Exchanged prisoners appeared, one of them the invaluable frontier fighter Daniel Morgan, who had been captured at Quebec on an ill-fated American invasion of Canada. This specialist in Indian fighting and rifle marksmanship took command of a Virginia regiment.

By summer, the army moved into Bucks County, Pennsylvania—where it was joined by the young Frenchman the Marquis de Lafayette. General Howe embarked thousands of his crack troops from New York, landed in the upper Chesapeake, and drove into Pennsylvania. Washington met them in September at Brandywine, a pitched battle along a hilly creek which was undoubtedly a British victory—but Nathanael Greene, hurrying a relief column to aid Gen. John Sullivan when a flank was turned, proved that his men could strike swiftly and hard. Once more, the troops from Maryland and Delaware had fought heroically. Among the best of the new British regiments to appear was the 23rd Foot—the Royal Welsh Fusileers.

Washington was not through. He made an audacious attack on the entrenched British at Germantown, and at first drove the enemy through fog and thick gunsmoke. Only a fatal halt to reduce a stone house slowed the assault, and when American regiments fired on each other in the confusion, there was retreat. American casualties were heavy, about a thousand men, but the army felt that it had come near victory. When fall came, Washington had 11,000 men, and the United States had been born, with the adoption of the Articles of Confederation. Washington went into camp at Valley Forge; there was doubt that the army of the new republic would survive the year.

At the end of a terrible winter the puny American army emerged to learn of the breath-taking alliance with France —and the regiments were more deadly, too, for Baron von Steuben had taught them Prussian discipline, in drill and battle tactics, skills they had never known. In June, 1778, Sir Henry Clinton abandoned Philadelphia, where his army had wintered, and ran for New York. In New Jersey, with his baggage stretched for miles along the roads, Washington caught him.

They fought at Monmouth, a fierce clash which passed as a drawn battle, since Washington held the ground and Clinton escaped with his wagons. An American victory was possibly thwarted by the treason or indecision of Gen. Charles

Lee, and only Washington's presence stemmed a panic of retreat. Here, on June 28, 1778, the main armies met for the last time in the north. The decision was left to other theaters.

In the preceding summer and fall, under direction of a spectacular officer, Gentleman Johnny Burgoyne, the British had suffered defeat more important than it appeared. Burgoyne had launched an offensive from Canada, drawn by the popular British scheme of cutting New England from the rest of the colonies. His force was to combine with two others after the capture of Fort Ticonderoga and sweep to Albany to clear the region of rebels.

One of the columns did not materialize, for Sir William Howe chose to remain far to the south, and the other was driven off by patriots of the region. In two battles at Freeman's Farm, or Saratoga, New York, Burgoyne was soundly beaten, and in the last engagement, surrounded, gave up his army of 5,000 of the best British and Hessian troops. The victorious American commander was Horatio Gates, but the decision had been won by Benedict Arnold and the leader of backwoods riflemen, Daniel Morgan.

Gates had become the American hero and been sent into the south at the insistence of Congress in 1780 to halt the new British tide in that quarter. He had been overwhelmed at the battle of Camden, South Carolina, in August, his army scattered, and its officers in flight.

It was to relieve Gates that Nathanael Greene had come into the Carolinas, in December, 1780—at a time when Washington's army had been idle for more than two years.

George III had been attracted by prospects in the south, where his governors reported many Loyalists ready to aid his armies. If the northern colonies must go, perhaps he could cling to the Carolinas, Virginia, and Georgia. The future was now uncertain, since French fleets were in America, and Spain had joined the war; also he had to send a fleet to relieve a siege at Gibraltar.

Henry Clinton commanded the southern expedition, but his heart was not in it; he had twice attempted to resign his post. In December, 1779, he sailed against Charleston, South Carolina, with 7,600 men. A stormy voyage cost him a shipload of heavy cannon, and two or three other ships were victims of American privateers. Most of his horses died or were drowned. Yet he besieged and conquered Charleston, where Gen. Benjamin Lincoln had 7,000 men and heavy guns.

The last hope of the city vanished when Lt. Col. Banastre Tarleton and his horsemen defeated American cavalry near the city; many Americans were killed after their surrender. Tarleton's troops were the Legion, recruited in America, about half cavalry and half infantry. The only regular troops attached were in one troop (twenty men) of the 17th Light Dragoons, who held their fellows in contempt, and clung to their green coats rather than wear the Legion scarlet. The Legion had appeared briefly in the north, chiefly in outpost and guerrilla warfare.

Clinton sailed north with a large part of his army to meet the threat of a French fleet, and Cornwallis was left to direct the campaign: Three columns would march into inland South Carolina, establish posts, and prepare a drive through North Carolina and Virginia. It was this force, of some 2,500, that conquered Gates and a greatly superior army at Camden.

Cornwallis remained in the interior; he advanced to Charlotte, North Carolina, but when bands of mountain riflemen destroyed the army of Tories under Maj. Patrick Ferguson at Kings Mountain in October, 1780, the British retreated.

Cornwallis went into winter camp in the village of Winnsboro, on the western frontier of South Carolina.

For the coming campaign, Cornwallis had about twenty-five hundred men, most of them veterans of northern fighting. His regiments included:

The 23rd Foot, the Royal Welsh Fusileers
The 33rd Foot, West Ridings
The 71st Highlanders
The 7th Foot
Tarleton's Legion

To face him, Greene found in Charlotte a mere 800 men, including the remnants of the First Maryland, into which was incorporated the Delaware troops, of little more than a company.

Other regulars were only the Legion of Lt. Col. Harry Lee, chiefly Virginia cavalry and mounted infantry, and fewer than 100 Virginia cavalry under Lt. Col. William Washington. Daniel Morgan, now a brigadier general, commanded a scouting force of frontier riflemen. Otherwise, the veterans of the earlier fighting were gone—but many of them were at home, awaiting the next crisis. Militia bands were constantly moving back and forth, bound to and from short terms of enlistment. In contrast to rigid British organization, there was chaos in the American camp. Yet these motley little regiments, men in buckskins and farm clothing mingling with a handful of Continental regulars, were of the sort who won high praise from a visiting French officer. Cromot duBourg, aide to Count Rochambeau in French headquarters, said of these unprepossessing soldiers:

"I cannot insist too strongly how I was surprised by the American Army. It is truly incredible that troops almost naked, poorly paid, and composed of old men and children and negroes should behave so well on the march and under fire."

British arms were vastly superior, by all conventional standards, but ordnance of both armies, with few exceptions, was almost primitive. Neither muskets nor cannon had been significantly improved for centuries, and as the Revolution opened, the warring nations lagged behind France in weapons development.

The standard British infantry arm was the Land Musket, made in long and short barrels, which afterward became famous as the Brown Bess. Its smooth iron barrel was 62 inches long in early models, but had been reduced to 44 and then to 39 inches. It was a sturdy gun designed for mass infantry fire at short range, without true aiming. Manuals prescribed a rate of fire of one round every fifteen seconds—but this was under ideal conditions.

The Brown Bess was reliable, fired a ball of about .75 caliber, and carried a bayonet. There were complaints of hammers breaking, but these had been improved over the years.

American muskets were modeled on these British arms, since they had been in wide use in the colonies. When war came, the States got a variety of arms from every possible source—confiscation, contract, production of local smiths, and purchase abroad. Massachusetts ordered muskets "equal in goodness with the King's new arms." Connecticut and Maryland imported barrels and locks and had local smiths to stock and mount them. Maryland opened a gunlock factory at Frederick in 1776.

Virginia was first to open a gun factory, at Fredericksburg in 1775, and also bought from private makers like James Hunter.

These American muskets were copies of the Brown Bess, about the same length and caliber; fittings were inferior, of iron rather than brass.

Within a few months, American troops began to prefer French muskets, which appeared through the blockade, shipped by the dummy French corporation of Roderique Hortalez *et. Cie.,* which smuggled arms to the rebels.

The muskets of this war had effective ranges of 80 to 100 yards—and could seldom hit a specific man-sized target at extreme range. They were fired in volleys, and reloaded in the open battlefield, often under fire. They were essentially iron tubes held in walnut stocks, pierced with a touchhole under the flintlock, so that a falling flint in the hammer could spurt a spark into a pan of powder, through the hole, to ignite the charge in the barrel. Paper cartridges were in use by both sides, and these were rammed down the barrel first, with ramrods, followed by musket balls. In most actions, muskets used fixed ammunition.

French muskets, similar to the Brown Bess, had improvements of value in the field: Barrels were banded firmly to the stock, and the hammers were held by rings, rather than the gooseneck of the Brown Bess. Range and rate of fire were about the same.

The German troops brought a variety of new weapons, but except for the Prussian models, the muskets were undependable. The most important German weapon was the short rifle used by the Yagers, picked troops who had been trained as foresters and huntsmen—and who soon inspired fear in the Americans with their marksmanship.

The most accurate of all infantry weapons was the American rifle developed by backwoods smiths on the frontiers of Pennsylvania and Kentucky—an elongated version of the old German rifles, used for providing meat and killing Indians. It was not the decisive weapon of the Revolution, but drew the world-wide attention of military men. The twelve rifle corps reporting to Washington at Boston in 1775 staged shooting matches in which one company put all of its shots in a 7-inch-square target at 250 yards. A British expert, Maj. George Hanger, wrote of an American rifleman who killed a horse at a range of 400 yards.

The rifle had been deadly at Saratoga, when the marksmen had the chance to fire from woodlands at exposed British targets, but it had only limited use in the north. It had serious disadvantages in infantry fighting, since it had no bayonet and was slow to load—it could be expected to fire about once a minute in battle. It used no fixed ammunition, and the powder charge was poured in from a horn, followed by a bullet wrapped in a square of greased buckskin, all tamped by a ramrod.

The rifle's shortcomings vexed George Washington, who once ordered Daniel Morgan's men to carry spears; he felt that the army had too many riflemen. The northern fighting had provided few opportunities for rifle corps to show their effectiveness. If supported by musket-firing infantry or cavalry, the long guns could damage the enemy at a great range, and on such terrain as Kings Mountain, the rifle was deadly. Snipers and outlying skirmishers would make it supreme.

The first artillery heard in America was French, fired from a fleet in 1565; by 1637 the Ancient & Honorable Artillery Company of Boston had been formed, but it was not until 1745, at the battle of Louisburg, that big guns appeared in full battle array. The forests of America hampered the art, and continued to do so through most of the Revolution.

Both armies used as their guide John Muller's *Treatise on Artillery*, an English text reprinted in Philadelphia in 1779. Muller had improved British gunnery in the 1760's, following the French lead, and given it better range by refining ornate design and reducing weight.

The field guns of the Revolution were light, usually firing 3-pound or 6-pound solid iron balls. They were drawn by teams of horses or oxen, often under civilian drivers, but on the battlefield were dragged into position by their crews with the use of ropes. The barrels were bronze or iron (as early as 1775 a Philadelphia foundry was turning out both). Boxes on the carriage held twenty-one rounds of ammunition—and they fired either solid shot, grapeshot, or case shot. Often, fixed ammunition was available—the gunpowder bag fixed to the cannon ball with a wooden round between them.

The barrels were smoothbore, with a touchhole near the rear. The powder was pushed in first, loose in a ladle, or in a bag, followed by a wad, and the ball. The effective range of these light guns was 600 to 800 yards, with disabling effect up to 900 yards. With the use of grape (packets of iron balls about 2 inches in diameter), they were quite deadly in the open field. The guns themselves weighed about eighty-five times as much as the balls they fired.

Gunpowder, often scarce, was black, sensitive to spark or flame, often ruined by absorption of moisture. It was made of six parts of saltpeter (potassium nitrate) to one part each of sulphur and charcoal by weight. The ignition of this mixture liberated smoky gases which abruptly occupied 300 times the space of the powder, and flung the ball from the barrel. Nine-pounder cannon well charged with powder would hurl balls at more than 1,000 feet per second.

The guns were tended by crews of seven or eight, and were ignited by use of a slow match—a three-strand cotton rope soaked in a saltpeter solution and lead acetate, so that it would burn no more than 4 or 5 inches an hour. Aiming was done with a gunner's quadrant, by then more than 400 years old, a device like a carpenter's square with a plumb bob hanging in a quarter-circle which was graduated to show the angle of elevation. By reading tables, gunners could raise or lower the barrel at each shot; each mark of the quadrant would change the range by one-tenth.

With these crude arms, and these wildly mismatched forces, Charles, Lord Cornwallis and Nathanael Greene, a fighting Quaker from Rhode Island, opened the southern campaign of 1781, which was to influence strongly the outcome of the American Revolution.

Cowpens
January 17, 1781

THERE WAS A COLD MISTING RAIN ALL DAY, AND THE GENeral's rheumatism was so painful that he did not stir his horse out of a slow walk. He came along at the tail of the procession. The scarecrow army marched twelve miles during the day, fording flooded creeks and climbing wooded hills in the back country of western South Carolina. It was Jan. 16, 1781. The enemy was close behind.

The General was not sure how many men were in ranks; no more than 800, and only a handful of them regulars of the Continental line—the remnants of a regiment from Maryland and a company from Delaware. They had been frightened from their breakfast by a report of the oncoming British, and left fires behind them, and food cooking. Men grumbled about their commander, who had seemed so stern lately when he hanged deserters in the camp, but was now running from the invaders as if he would never stop.

They halted near sundown when the rain paused. It was a good camp—a long grassy glade amid open woodlands which had been cleared by cattle kept in the place for many years. It was called Hannah's Cowpens, a lost drover's camp on the old Cherokee trading trail. The ground sloped upward for about 700 yards to a crest, behind which was a swale with a second hill beyond. The trees were large—oaks, poplars, chestnuts, and a few pines. Broad River was about six miles away, out of sight in the towering forest. A scouting party returned to the General with word that the river was too high for fording, and he thought of escape no more. If he crossed the river, he knew, at least half the militia would run away from the British. Here, they might be so fearful of the enemy that they would turn and fight; there was no escape.

Officers near the General were astonished by his reaction; the commander looked at the ground as if he had not seen it before, taking note of the upward slope through the scattered trees, and the swale behind the ridge, where standing troops could be hidden. He said impatiently: "I'll whip them here or lay down my bones."

One officer thought he had lost his quick temper, and was tired of being chased by Lt. Col. Banastre Tarleton and "the damned British." Others looked at the position and saw that the enemy cavalry could quickly encircle both flanks, while the infantry charged the hill with its bayonets. It seemed a poor spot to test the little army.

No one saw the General when, a bit after dark, he walked a few yards into the woods and climbed a tree. He confessed later: "I poured out my soul in prayer for protection." Later in the night, no one suspected that he had been praying.

The General was Daniel Morgan, the son of Welsh parents, born in New Jersey or Pennsylvania—no one could be sure. He was forty-five years old this winter, an old woodsman and wagon driver who had been with the Braddock expedition as a boy and seen the British regulars massacred by Indian warriors. By family tradition, his sister was Sarah Morgan, mother of a frontiersman who would rise to fame: Daniel Boone. Morgan's back was laced with old scars, a reminder of 500 lashes applied by a British Army disciplinarian; almost half his teeth were gone, shot out by an Indian marksman in a frontier ambush. Except for learning acquired from his wife, Abigail Curry, Morgan was untutored; in his youth he had been a hard-drinking, fist-fighting wild man, a strong, huge boy whose wandering finally ceased when he settled near Winchester, in the Shenandoah Valley of Virginia.

He had commanded the first company of riflemen in the American army at the outbreak of the Revolution—formed, trained, and in three weeks marched it the 400 miles from Winchester to Boston, where George Washington shook the hand of every man. He had marched with Arnold and Montgomery to Quebec, and was captured after his troops stormed the heights. He had come from prison to fight once more at Saratoga, but though he had played a major role in that American victory, he got no mention in the dispatches. He lost his riflemen, and was given a militia brigade instead, still with the rank of colonel. He went home to nurse his rheumatism and his wounded pride. Only when the British general, Lord Charles Cornwallis, began driving through the Carolinas, did Morgan return to war. Now, at last, he had been made a brigadier general, to give him rank over the backwoods colonels in whose country he fought.

Only a few nights earlier he had written his chief, Maj. Gen. Nathanael Greene:

The enemy is greatly superior in numbers and my distance from the main army will enable C. to detach so superior a force against me as to render it essential to avoid coming to action. Nor will this always be in my power. . . . It is beyond the art of man to keep the militia from straggling.

The commander had replied with the air of a man made cautious by bitter experience:

. . . It is my wish that you hold your ground if possible, for I foresee the disagreeable consequences of retreat. . . . Colonel Tarleton is said to be on his way to pay you a visit. I doubt not he will have a decent reception and a proper dismission, and I am happy to find you have taken every precaution against a surprise. . . .

It is not my wish you should come to action unless you have a manifest superiority. . . . Put nothing to the hazard. A retreat may be disagreeable but not disgraceful. Regard not the opinions of the day. It is not our business to risk too much. . . .

In short, Morgan was on his own. There would be no specific orders from Greene, who lay in camp with the main southern army, about 140 miles to the east, on the Pee Dee River.

In the camp at the Cowpens, men in ranks saw Morgan in a new light. Thomas Young, a boy volunteer who rode with the troopers of Lt. Col. William Washington, had been fretting: "We were very anxious for battle, and many a hearty curse had been vented against General Morgan during that day's march for retreating, as we thought, to avoid a battle."

After the troops had eaten, Young began to suspect that

he had misjudged his man: "He went among the volunteers, helped them fix their swords, joked with them about their sweethearts, told them to keep in good spirits and the day would be ours. And long after I had laid down, he was going among the soldiers encouraging them and telling them that the Old Wagoner would crack his whip over Ban Tarleton in the morning, as sure as they lived."

Morgan went to every fire among the companies of militiamen in the camp, shouting so that hundreds could hear his voice: "Just hold up your heads, boys, three rounds of fire, and you're free, and when you go back home, how the old folks will bless you and the girls will kiss you." Morgan got no sleep during the night.

He ordered every militia captain to see that each man had twenty-four rounds of ammunition before he went to sleep. He gave out passwords for the night, hoping that they would inspire the men: "Fire" and "Sword."

Several patrols went out to scout the trail over which they had come, looking for the enemy. Wagons creaked off toward Broad River with the skimpy baggage, and messengers were sent on horseback in an effort to hasten the militia bands which still came in through the woodlands.

Colonel Andrew Pickens came with more than 100 men; he was a seasoned guerrilla leader from South Carolina, trained in frontier fighting from youth. He was called by the Indians Skyagunsta, the Border Wizard Owl. Several other parties trailed in, all asking for powder or lead, and for news of the enemy. The reinforcements were in high spirits, and most of them brought fresh tales of atrocities committed by the British, who were burning and looting over a wide area. The newcomers improved morale in camp.

Another band was led by Maj. James McCall, from

Georgia; his forty-five men carried homemade swords and were mounted on wiry backwoods ponies. Morgan sent them to William Washington as support—so that now the Virginian who led the Third Dragoon Regiment boasted a command of 125 troopers.

Late in the night two militia colonels raced in with a report: Tarleton had crossed Thicketty Creek, just half a dozen miles away, and they had counted his strength—1,150 men. An hour before daylight, in bitter cold, Morgan went among the sleeping troops to rouse them: "Boys, get up! Banny is coming!" The men cooked at their fires, and soon went into battle lines the General pointed out to them:

On the crest of the slope he posted the main line, the Maryland regiment, the Delaware men, and two companies of Virginians led by Captains Triplett and Tate. Both the latter companies were old Continentals whose terms had expired, and who had re-enlisted; Tate's men were the Augusta Riflemen. On their outer right flank was a small party of Georgians under Major Beatty. Commander of this line was Lt. Col. John Eager Howard, of Maryland.

About 150 yards below this main line, and to its front, were volunteers from the Carolinas and Georgia, under Colonel Pickens. The right of this line was commanded by Maj. Charles McDowell, a Kings Mountain veteran, who had North Carolinians; with him, and to his right, were South Carolinians under a militia colonel, Brannon. And 150 yards farther down the slope was a thin screen of skirmishers, all riflemen, about 150 strong. The left flank of the skirmish line was a Georgia company of Maj. John Cunningham, with more of the South Carolina riflemen on the far left. Cunningham's men in particular were tried veterans, the survivors of the corps of the celebrated border fighter, Col. Elijah Clarke, who was now recovering from wounds.

To the rear of the whole infantry position, behind the hill, was a swale, a grassy area about 80 yards wide, where the cavalry of Washington and McCall were placed to guard the horses of the militiamen and come out in support when called. These riders could stand in their stirrups and see down the long slope over the heads of the infantry to the spot where the enemy was expected.

Morgan faced his men to cheer them as if they were about to engage in some backwoods game. To the riflemen in the front line he said, "Let's see who are the most entitled to be called brave men, the boys of Carolina or those of Georgia." He gave Pickens's militia a rousing speech, pounding his fist in the palm of his hand, asked them to behave as bravely as they always had, to pour in two fires at killing range, and then to retire. He reminded them that he had never been defeated in open battle, and at last told them to "ease their joints" and wait.

The General rode up to Howard's line and shouted even more loudly: "My friends in arms, my dear boys, I ask you to remember Saratoga, Monmouth, Paoli, Brandywine, and this day you must play your part for your honor and liberty's cause." The men in ranks seemed to expect such a harangue, for there was cheering from the regulars, and one officer thought them "all in good spirits and very willing to fight."

The long, spare Colonel Pickens, a devout Presbyterian of such reserve that it was said he held each word thoughtfully in his hands before releasing it, also joined the oratory briefly. He told his militia that they might hide behind trees to fire, but that they were not to shoot until the enemy was within 30 yards. Morgan warned the regulars to expect the militia of Pickens to retreat behind them, and that they should not be alarmed by this movement.

Morgan rode to a spot behind the main line, on a flank, and sat his horse quietly, with an air of confidence as if he led a great force of the Continental veterans—and as if he had never seen the militia run like rabbits at the sight of scarlet uniforms.

As he waited, looking down the slope of this remarkably open and accessible battle site, Morgan may have thought of those who would criticize his choice of ground, to whom he would one day reply:

> I would not have had a swamp in view of my militia on any consideration; they would have made for it, and nothing could have detained them from it. And as to covering my wings, I knew my adversary and was perfectly sure I would have nothing but downright fighting. As to retreat, it was the very thing I wished to cut off all hope of. I would have thanked Tarleton had he surrounded me with cavalry. It would have been better than placing my own men in the rear to shoot down those who broke from the ranks. When men are forced to fight, they will sell their lives dearly.

The General and the army waited. The lines were complete soon after dawn, and there was no relief from the cold until, just before eight o'clock, the last of the scouts fled through them, and the enemy had come.

Lieutenant Colonel Banastre Tarleton had come to America in 1775, with a commission bought for him by his father, a rich Liverpool merchant. The boy commander had quickly made a reputation as a ruthless chief of cavalry and rose to brigade major in the northern campaigns. When the British offensive turned southward in 1780 and drove inland through South Carolina, the Oxford-trained Tarleton led the cavalry of Cornwallis's army.

He conducted total warfare in the Carolinas, already torn by civil strife. Tarleton taught the Whigs no-quarter fighting. In one border skirmish his horsemen sabered scores of militiamen after they had surrendered, and "Tarleton's Quarters" had become a Whig battle cry as his green-coated troopers rode through the country, burning houses, seizing food and supplies and liberating Negro slaves.

A Tory scout of the campaign described the striking "wild blade" in these words:

A picture of a man he was! Rather below the middle height, and with a face almost femininely beautiful . . . a form that was a perfect model of manly strength and vigor. Without a particle of superfluous flesh, his rounded limbs and full broad chest seemed moulded from iron, yet displaying all the elasticity which usually accompanies elegance of proportion. His dress was a jacket and breeches of white linen, fitted to his form with the utmost exactness. Boots of russet leather were halfway up the leg, the broad tops were turned down, the heels garnished with spurs of an immense size. On his head was a low crowned hat, curiously formed from the snow-white feathers of the swan.

On the first day of 1781 Lord Cornwallis wrote Tarleton from his camp at Winnsboro, South Carolina:

Pass Broad River with the Legion and the first battalion of the 71st as soon as possible. . . . If Morgan . . . is anywhere within your reach, I should wish you to push him to the utmost.

Tarleton asked for more men, and Cornwallis gave them;

the British chief had 1,500 reinforcements on the way from the South Carolina coast, under Maj. Gen. Alexander Leslie.

In addition to his own Legion, 550 of both infantry and cavalry, Tarleton had 200 of the Seventy-first Regiment, 200 of the Seventh Regiment, and 50 of the crack 17th Light Dragoons. Including a few artillerymen to man his two guns, he had almost 1,100 men in the column. He wrote Cornwallis: "I must either destroy Morgan's corps, or push it before me over Broad River, toward Kings Mountain." He suggested that Cornwallis push up the east side of Broad River with the main army, and the commander agreed. Tarleton proceeded thereafter on the premise that Cornwallis was moving steadily on a parallel course northward.

Tarleton sent a final request: "Bring up my baggage, but no women. . . . Escort to me three puncheons of rum and some salt; and upon their arrival, I will move."

Cornwallis replied to his favorite: "You have exactly done what I wished you to do and understood my intentions perfectly." Cornwallis lagged back, waiting for Leslie and his reinforcements.

Tarleton felt his way toward Morgan, who was now reported to have 1,200 men, with more militia thronging in daily. The British crossed rain-swollen creeks and, on Jan. 14, crossed both the Enoree and Tyger Rivers. The next day, with the advice of native spies, they used one of the numerous fords of the Pacolet River, a tributary of Broad River, and, shaking off enemy scouts, they found at a place known as Grindal's Shoals Morgan's abandoned camp of log huts, where the fires still burned.

Dragoons and scouts pushed ahead and followed the American trail until darkness fell; some of them returned with word that Morgan had left the main path and lunged into the country, crossing Thicketty Creek. A captured American militia colonel gave Tarleton good news he could scarcely believe: The victim was ready to make a stand. The British column rested for a few hours.

At 3 A.M. on Jan. 17 Tarleton left his baggage wagons behind, with orders to go farther to the rear. He put three companies of light infantry in front, the infantry of his Legion and the Seventh Regiment next, then the two cannon and the men of the Seventy-first. The rear was covered by cavalry and mounted infantry. It was slow work on the narrow trail, and the crossing of a flooded creek in the darkness snarled the column.

The vanguard had luck in the half-light near dawn, stumbling into an American mounted patrol and riding down a couple of pickets after a chase. Tarleton now knew that Morgan was waiting; he called in guides and asked for a description of the country in the American rear. He rode to the edge of a clearing and gazed up at the lines of the enemy, smiling with satisfaction as he studied the ground: "An open wood was certainly as proper a place for action as any [I] could desire; America does not produce many more suitable to the nature of the troops. The situation of the enemy was desperate in case of misfortune. . . ."

Tarleton hurried his men with a trace of impatience. The British had marched five miles since three o'clock, and some of the troops had been put to hard physical labor in the passage of the rough country—pushing wagons when they mired in the mud. The newcomers did not know the ground and were in some confusion. Their opponents looked down on them from prepared lines on a landscape familiar to them, having eaten breakfast at leisure and made ready their arms and ammunition. Tarleton did not hesitate so much as to call a consultation with his officers. He sent the dragoons of the Legion dashing up among the trees to drive off the American skirmishers; when the green-jacketed troopers were quite near the enemy position, the rifles flamed; several saddles were empty when the dragoons returned to Tarleton. Part of the outer line of Americans had been driven back, but the main portion was unmoved.

Still Tarleton sensed no danger. He was cautious enough to form his line out of range of the deadly rifles, some 400 to 500 yards from the enemy; he rode busily down a forming line of attack in his green cloak, a long plume tossing over his brass helmet. He placed the two brass three-pounders in the line and ordered them to open; for a few minutes they hurled shot against the slope, but there was little effect beyond the toppling of some tree limbs.

The British formed promptly. Tarleton ordered them to leave everything they carried except arms and ammunition. the light infantry was filed off to the right until it reached a point opposite the far American flank. The infantrymen of the Legion went in next to them, and when these units had made a straight line, they advanced within 300 yards of the Americans under cover of the cannon fire.

Tarleton watched the enemy more closely while this move was made; he estimated that the Americans had about 1,000 men in the first line, with 500 Continentals, 300 back-woodsmen, and about 120 of Washington's cavalry to the rear. Even these odds did not impress him.

He sent the Seventh Regiment into line at the left of the Legion infantry, and on each flank of the lengthened front he placed a group of fifty of his Legion dragoons, each group under a captain. All were now in place, in one long line of scarlet and green coats. Behind them Tarleton kept a reserve

—the battalion of the Seventy-first Regiment and about two hundred cavalry. This reserve was about 150 yards behind the assault line and slightly to the left of the Seventh Regiment's flank.

The commander was pleased by the work of the men as they got into position: "The animation of the officers and the alacrity of the soldiers afforded the most promising assurances of success."

A few Americans slipped out from the front line and sniped at the forming British. Some of the green troops of the Seventh Regiment, the newer recruits, began a nervous fire in reply. When that was suppressed by officers, the long colorful line of figures stepped out toward the enemy. Tarleton watched them proudly from the rear: "The troops moved on in as good a line as troops could move at open files."

But the lines began to snarl as they came within range of the waiting backwoodsmen. The first rifles opened. The British raised a cheer.

Morgan galloped among his men, bellowing: "They give us the British halloo, boys. Give 'em the Indian halloo, by God!" There was a chorus of war whoops from above as the riflemen fired. Officers called continually for the men to hold their fire, and then, when the British were in range: "The epaulet men, boys! Pick off the epaulets." Officers began to fall in the British line, but the press continued up the hill in discipline typical of the redcoats.

Within a few minutes, when it had come quite near the line of McDowell and Cunningham, the British line noticeably slowed for the first time; the militia fired a first volley, which seemed to Morgan "a heavy and galling fire." The British halted to reload, and there was confusion in some companies as men on both sides raced through the ceremony of pouring powder and ramming shot, priming the pieces for another round. When the British came on after a second general volley, the American militiamen retreated ahead of them.

McDowell and Cunningham led the withdrawal with skill; men halted behind trees, reloading as they went, and many fired during this time. There was no panic; many of these men had fought in the victory over Maj. Patrick Ferguson at Kings Mountain about two months earlier. They fell back in two groups, one of which settled into line with the militia of Colonel Pickens, ready for a second stand; the other group circled the left flank and went out of sight behind the hill where the Continentals waited. Here the riflemen were re-formed. Out in front, the British moved up to meet the second line.

Firing became heavier. One soldier in the militia line was James P. Collins, a Kings Mountain veteran who often became ill when he saw bloodshed. He was swallowing hard at the spectacle: "The enemy came in full view. The sight, to me at least, seemed somewhat imposing. They halted for a short time, then advanced as if certain of victory."

Thomas Young of the cavalry, who had come into the infantry line, was also impressed by the enemy: "It was the most beautiful line I ever saw." Morgan now rode down the line, urging his men to hold their ground and wait. Young wrote that: "He galloped along, cheering his men and telling them not to fire until we could see the whites of their eyes. Every officer was crying 'Don't fire!' for it was a hard matter to keep us from it."

Pickens held his line firm. He ordered men to fire by regiments, to provide cover for those who were reloading, and this volume of fire slowed the enemy. For a few minutes the two lines exchanged fire in the open, the pulse of the battle following the slow process of reloading and firing; men fell more rapidly in Tarleton's line.

The enemy had been delayed in front of Pickens for almost half an hour in a steady exchange of fire, when the British at last came within about 40 yards of the militiamen, halted under perfect control of their officers, and fired a mass volley. Most of them fired high, and bullets from the Brown Bess muskets hissed through and into the trees (more than fifty years later a visitor found their bullets, as much as 30 feet high in the trees).

With their muskets empty the British gave a cheer and lunged uphill with their bayonets. Some of Pickens's men broke for the rear at a run, frightened by sight of the glittering enemy steel and memories of the tales of veterans. Pickens held most of his men to an orderly retreat by shouting, and these men went "with haste" but with a show of discipline to the rear of the Continentals. Pickens put them into place on the right flank of the main line. Those who had fled had the longest route to travel, obliquely across the front of the Continentals, and before they reached the rear, they were struck by British horsemen.

A Captain Ogilvie, who led the dragoon party on the right flank of Tarleton, ordered a charge as soon as he saw militiamen running. The Englishmen were soon among the flying backwoodsmen, but in the charge their ranks were scattered by the rough terrain and the trees, and became disorganized in the midst of their victory.

James Collins retained a vivid memory of these moments as the line of Pickens broke: "We gave the enemy one fire; when they charged us with their bayonets, we gave way and retreated for our horses. Tarleton's cavalry pursued us. 'Now,' thought I, 'my hide is in the loft.'

"Just as we got to our horses, they overtook us and began to make a few hacks at some, however without doing much injury."

Most of this action was beyond the sight of men in the infantry lines on the slope, but Lieutenant Colonel Washington, watching from his rear position, spurred up to ask Howard for permission to charge.

Washington was a short, powerful man of twenty-seven with an angular and none-too-handsome face, a distant cousin of George Washington. He rode as recklessly as the youngest of his troopers; he had been born in Stafford County, Virginia, and trained for the ministry, but enlisted as soon as war came, becoming a captain of infantry. He was wounded at Trenton, when the Hessians were surprised. Only in the south, when the army was desperately in need of cavalry, had Washington been converted into a commander of horse.

Howard quickly nodded to Washington, and the Virginian motioned his troop to the attack. The riders of James McCall led the rush. James Collins saw the clash:

"Col. Washington's cavalry was among them like a whirlwind, and the poor fellows began to keel from their horses without being able to remount. The shock was so sudden and so violent that they could not stand it and immediately betook themselves to flight. There was no time to rally, and they appeared to be as hard to stop as a drove of wild Choctaw steers going to a Pennsylvania market. In a few moments the clashing of swords was out of hearing and quickly out of sight."

Tarleton had lost one wing of the screening dragoons for his battle line.

There was a brief quarrel in the British command as the wing of Pickens's line retreated; Major McArthur, who commanded Tarleton's reserve, argued for a charge of all the cavalry, but the commander overruled him. The moment was now lost. Tarleton turned to the infantry, which appeared to have won the field thus far, despite the furor on the left flank of the enemy.

The British line was now exposed to the fire of the American Continentals, who fired slowly and steadily. More officers fell in the attacking file. Tarleton called up the infantry reserve, the battalion of the Seventy-first, the Highlanders. These men filed up on the American right flank, and were ordered to hold their fire until safely past the Seventh Regiment, and they moved into position with a parade-ground calm and precision. The British regimental bands played as the lines drew together. Except for his cavalry reserve, all of Tarleton's force was committed.

The British line was now longer than the American and began to lap around the right flank of Howard's line. The young officer rode to the threatened spot.

John Eager Howard was heir to a Maryland fortune which included Belvedere, a great town house in Baltimore, as well as the estate outside the city, where he had been born. He was a descendant of a refugee from the fighting against James II. Howard had joined George Washington's army at twenty-three, fought at White Plains and Germantown, and endured the winter at Valley Forge. In the preceding August his Maryland regiments, the core of the army of Horatio Gates, had been decimated in the disastrous defeat at Camden, South Carolina, though they had stood fast in the first flight of the American militia rabble. Today, in command of Morgan's major force, Howard was twenty-eight years old.

Howard saw that there was only an instant for decision: "Seeing my right flank was exposed to the enemy, I attempted to change the front of Wallace's company [Virginia regulars who had served one term and returned as militia]; in doing it, some confusion ensued, and first a part, and then the whole of the company commenced a retreat. The officers along the line seeing this, and supposing that orders had been given for a retreat, faced their men about and moved off. Morgan . . . quickly rode up.

" 'Have they whipped you?' Morgan said.

" 'Do men marching like that look as if they're beaten?'

" 'Have them follow me,' Morgan said. 'When they get to where I'll be standing, have them face about and fire.' "

Morgan rode for about fifty paces, according to his later memory, down the back of their hillside, across the grassy swale and up the next slope. He pointed out the place to Howard and rode among men of the flank shouting: "Stand and fire, men! Just one more volley. Old Morgan's never been whipped."

The field was now marked with pockets of confusion, but the American position was still unbroken, though it had sagged to the rear. Both cavalry and infantry were skirmishing in the melee.

Howard worked with his company officers on the new hillside: "In a minute we had a perfect line. The enemy were now very near us. Our men commenced a very destructive fire, which they little expected, and a few rounds occasioned great disorder in their ranks. While in this confusion I ordered a charge with the bayonet, which order was obeyed with great alacrity."

This British attack on the main line had now consumed about a quarter of an hour, a swift and roaring passage in which musket fire went on ceaselessly through banks of smoke now lying on the field.

William Washington had seen the British breaking ranks as they pressed nearer Howard's position, obviously convinced that one bayonet charge would scatter the apprehensive Americans. He sent a rider to Morgan with a message: "They're coming on like a mob. Give them one fire and I'll charge them." The cavalry was gathered on the flank, ready when Morgan gave the word. The horsemen broke into a trot just as Howard's infantrymen plunged down the slope into their unexpected bayonet charge. No one on the field could remember Americans charging British regulars with bayonets in an open engagement.

The British file abruptly disintegrated. It had lost its solid front in the act of charging; it was astonished by the wild charge of the enemy, led by the regulars of Maryland and Delaware; it was turned on its right by the charge of Washington's horsemen; it was enveloped on the left by a simultaneous rush from the militia of Pickens, who had re-formed and now bobbed up at the precise moment to join in a general charge. There was no place for the British to turn, and the disciplined units became a helpless mob, virtually surrounded.

Tarleton, who watched a few yards in the rear, was thunderstruck: "An unexpected fire at this instant from the Americans, who came about as they were retreating, stopped the British, and threw them into confusion. Exertions to make them advance were useless. The part of the cavalry which had not been engaged fell likewise into disorder, and an unaccountable panic extended itself along the whole line. The

Americans, who before thought they had lost the action, taking advantage of the present situation, advanced upon the British troops, and augmented their astonishment. A general flight ensued."

Tarleton could find no rational explanation for the sudden loss of confidence in his ranks, and the scene puzzled him for years afterward: "The defeat . . . must be ascribed either to the bravery or good conduct of the Americans; to the loose manner of forming which had always been practiced by the King's troops in America; or to some unforeseen event, which may throw terror into the most disciplined soldiers, or counteract the best-concerted designs."

When shouting and flailing with his sword did not halt the beginning panic, Tarleton sent a messenger to his cavalry: They were to form on the American right and check the charge, while Tarleton rallied the infantry in front of the cannon. The cavalry fled, and most of the riders were soon out of his sight. The infantrymen did not heed his shouts: "Neither promises nor threats could gain their attention; they surrendered or dispersed, and abandoned the guns to the artillerymen, who defended them for some time with exemplary resolution."

The gunners fought the Americans hand to hand until all were killed or wounded; none of these Britons ran.

Tarleton rode among a few of the cavalry reserve and persuaded them to follow him. More than 200 had now fled. He had only fourteen officers and forty horsemen of the mounted force to stand off the oncoming enemy, which was spread over the field. Tarleton's horse was shot from beneath him. He caught another in a general retreat through the woodlands.

Tarleton made a final gallant effort; he led his fifty-four

men in a headlong charge against Washington's superior cavalry, checked it briefly, but was soon beaten back by force of
numbers: "The loss sustained was in proportion to the danger
of the enterprise."

In the center of the field, where the British began throwing their muskets to the ground in surrender, Americans
shouted, "Tarleton's Quarters!" with the intention of butch-
ering their enemies. Howard stopped them by riding down
the line calling: "Give them quarter, men! Quarter!" If British were killed after they held up hands in surrender, it did
not creep into the scanty records of the engagement. Howard
barely averted a massacre, or had that impression:

"In the pursuit I was led toward the right, in among the
71st, who were broken into squads, and as I called to them to
surrender, they laid down their arms, and the officers delivered up their swords. Captain Duncanson, of the 71st
Grenadiers, gave me his sword and stood by me. Upon getting
on my horse, I found him pulling at my saddle, and he nearly
unhorsed me. I expressed my displeasure and asked him what
he was about. The explanation was that they had orders to
give no quarter, and they did not expect any; and as my men
were coming up, he was afraid they would use him ill. I admitted his excuse and put him under the care of a sergeant."

When the British line fell apart, Howard was the first
field officer to catch sight of the enemy guns and called to
a Captain Ewing in his ranks: "Take the guns!" Another
captain, Anderson, who overheard the order, raced with
Ewing's company for the two brass pieces. Anderson won by
vaulting the last few yards, driving the blade of his espontoon
into the ground and soaring through the air to the side of the
gun. There was a fierce struggle with the gunners before the
cannon were taken.

When Morgan rode up to inspect the guns, he found them familiar; these had been taken from General Burgoyne in the victory at Saratoga, lost to the British by Thomas Sumter in a skirmish at Blackstocks, South Carolina, and were now retaken in the surprise victory in the backwoods.

More than 500 infantrymen had thrown down their muskets at Howard's offer of quarters, and were now prisoners, being herded off the littered field. Looting of the dead and wounded had already begun. Of Tarleton's force only the cavalry had escaped.

Tarleton galloped down a country road in the wake of his 200 hurrying horsemen, accompanied by the small party of survivors from his final counterattack.

William Washington led the chase with such impatience that he was soon far in front of his cavalry force, virtually alone. The British hung back in an effort to cut off the American leader, and there was a brief sword fight in the roadway. An officer who whirled his saber at Washington had the blow parried by a Sergeant Major Perry, who in turn wounded the Englishman. When another Briton thrust at Washington, he was shot down with a pistol by a fourteen-year-old Virginia bugler. By a story brought back to camp in the night, Washington broke a sword in a hand-to-hand duel with Tarleton, and his horse was shot by the enemy leader. Tarleton was also reported to have been wounded in the head by a sword cut.

The British broke off and outdistanced Washington, and escaped when the Americans briefly took the wrong road in pursuit. Tarleton reached the Pacolet River a few minutes in advance of the enemy and forced a guide, one Goudelock, to guide him across the stream near his home. While the British were fording within a few hundred yards, Washington arrived, but Goudelock's wife told him that the British had already crossed the stream, in an effort to save her husband. Washington turned back after a chase of twenty-four miles.

The British baggage, which had waited in wagons about fifteen miles from the battle site, was burned. Its guard had been composed of a few men from each unit in the attacking force, under command of a Lieutenant Fraser of the Seventy-first Regiment. There were conflicting reports of its loss: Fraser had burned the wagons when fleeing Tories brought word of defeat at the Cowpens, and hurried for camp; Tory backwoodsmen had looted the wagons and were driven off by Tarleton, who mistook them for Americans; and, Tarleton himself reported, he had burned the stores after driving off American raiders to prevent their loss. The remnants of the British army, at any rate, were in full flight, without baggage.

Daniel Morgan rode over the field when quiet returned. He had fought for little more than an hour with his small force, which was more than half militia, against more than 1,000 well-trained British troops, most of whom were regulars. The General was so elated that he hoisted a nine-year-old drummer and kissed him.

Morgan had lost 12 killed and 60 wounded. There were 110 British bodies, 10 of them officers. Of the 702 captives, 200 had been wounded; the last of the prisoners were being rounded up in the woodlands nearby as Morgan inspected the ground. Of the British prisoners, 29 were officers. Among the captives were 70 Negroes liberated by the British for use as servants to officers. Some believed that the enemy officers, grown accustomed to luxury, had thus contributed to the defeat.

The two cannon were most welcome of all, but Morgan had also taken 800 muskets, 35 baggage wagons which had been close in the British rear, 100 good dragoon horses, regimental colors, much ammunition, a traveling forge, and "all their music."

An exact accounting of the casualties would never be made, and the figures remained in controversy. Tarleton made light of his losses despite his obvious meeting with disaster, but the official British returns dwindled by 784 men from the report of Jan. 15 to Feb. 1, and with the addition of Negroes, the American claims of a British loss of 850 were largely substantiated.

There was only an excited survey in the hour of victory, for it was clearly the most striking American victory of the war and was to be hailed as the most imitated, and best-fought, of the patriot victories of the rebellion. The country would soon ring with Morgan's praises, and Congress would strike medals and award ceremonial swords in honor of the day.

Analysis of the battle would require years, but Morgan and his officers did not regard it as an inscrutable mystery: The ground had been boldly chosen, defended by experienced men who had seen battle or frontier skirmishing over many years; the troops had been handled simply, with calm common sense, with respect for advantages of the landscape. A triple line of men had overcome a body of supposedly superior troops which was deployed in a thin single line without support when the crisis came.

The British attack had not only been impetuously delivered; Tarleton's alignment of the men, though orthodox, had placed them in potential danger from the start. When that commander wrote of the action six years later, it was with a note of wonder, but there was a criticism of the orthodox British tactic of spreading infantry in a long battle line—a tactic he employed during that morning without betraying the least lack of confidence:

"The extreme extension of the files always exposed the British regiments and corps, and would, before this unfortunate affair, have been attended with detrimental effect, had not the multiplicity of lines with which they generally fought rescued them from such imminent danger. If infantry who are formed very open, and only two deep, meet with opposition, they can have no stability: But when they experience an unexpected shock, confusion will ensue, and flight, without immediate support, must be the inevitable consequence."

Morgan devoted little time to study of the battle. He did not so much as wait for Washington to return from his chase. He knew that Cornwallis, lying twenty-five miles away to the southeast, would have word of the battle within five or six hours, and that the main army of the British would lose no time in striking. While his men were still hooting triumphantly on the field, Morgan had his officers form the line of march for a northward movement. He and Cornwallis were roughly equidistant from the meeting of their two roads, at Ramsour's Mill on the south fork of the Catawba River, just across the North Carolina line. Encumbered by his prisoners, Morgan must hurry if he was to win the race to that junction.

Morgan paroled the British officers, on their oaths not to enter the fighting until exchanged; he took a careful list of their names and ranks. He left Colonel Pickens with some local militia to care for the wounded and bury the dead. The enemy wounded who were unable to march were left under captured British tents, under a guard and a flag of truce. Enemy baggage was burned, except for arms and ammunition.

The wounded were left in charge of Dr. Richard Pindell, a volunteer surgeon with Morgan's force, who worked on men of both armies while soldiers gathered muskets and other supplies from the field.

It was about noon when these things were done. The march began. Morgan's column was lengthened by the file of Negroes as well as the prisoners, and the baggage wagons, full of piled muskets and ammunition, made progress slow. The prisoners were about two-thirds of Morgan's strength as he moved northward. The troops reached the Cherokee Ford, an old crossing of Broad River, by late afternoon, forded, and camped on the far bank. The General did not leave the water's edge until he had seen the captured cannon safely across. The rest was brief in this camp; Morgan had them moving before daylight.

William Washington's cavalry soon caught up with the column, but Colonel Pickens did not report until next day with a badly dwindled force; many of his militiamen had been dismissed at Cowpens. Late in the day of Jan. 18 scouts reported to Morgan: Cornwallis had not yet moved. Morgan was relieved, but did not slow the pace, for rains threatened to raise the rivers ahead of him and perhaps bar his way at unfordable stream crossings.

It was two days after the battle, when he paused in camp at Cane Creek on the wilderness trail, before Morgan sent a report to Nathanael Greene:

> The troops I have the honor to command have been so fortunate as to obtain a complete victory over a detachment from the British army, commanded by Lieut. Col. Tarleton. . . . It, perhaps, would be well to remark, for the honor of American arms, that although the progress of this corps was marked with burning and devastation, and although they

waged the most cruel warfare, not a man was killed, wounded, or even insulted after he surrendered. Had not Britons during this contest received so many lessons of humanity, I should flatter myself that this might teach them a little, but I fear they are incorrigible. . . .

From our force being composed of such a variety of corps, a wrong judgment may be formed of our numbers. We fought only eight hundred men, two-thirds of which were militia. The British, with their baggage-guard, were not less than one thousand one hundred and fifty, and these veteran troops. Their own officers confess that they fought one thousand and thirty-seven.

Such was the inferiority of our numbers that our success must be attributed to the justice of our cause and the bravery of our troops. My wishes would induce me to mention the name of every sentinel in the corps I have the honor to command. In justice to the bravery and good conduct of the officers, I have taken the liberty to enclose a list of their names, from a conviction that you will be pleased to introduce such characters to the world.

Morgan enclosed a long summary of the action, a list of casualties on both sides (excluding those of Pickens), and the list of British officers he had paroled. This went off by an express rider, Morgan's aide, Maj. Edward Giles. He had a ride of 130 miles or more to the southeast, where Greene waited with the main southern army in camp at the High Hills of Santee, on the Pee Dee River not far from the later town of Cheraw, South Carolina. Giles had a further adventure ahead, for after he delivered the news to Greene, he rode far northward, to Philadelphia, with a stop at Richmond, Virginia, with word for Governor Jefferson. Once there, however, he forgot himself, and when Jefferson finally got the dispatch, Giles had written on it: "Major Giles presents his compliments to Governor Jefferson and begs he would excuse his omitting to deliver him this letter. He was so engrossed with the pleasure of imparting good news, that he lost his recollection."

Morgan continued to send scouting parties to check the position of Cornwallis, for in the face of danger from Cornwallis, and with Greene at such a distance as to make communications slow, there was no plan of campaign beyond Morgan's determination to escape with the prisoners. On the second day he split his column in two, sending the prisoners under a guard of Pickens's men and some of Washington's cavalry over a more westerly route which would lead them to the Island Ford of the smaller branch of the Catawba. Morgan led the larger body toward Sherrill's Ford of the Catawba. He hoped that Greene would meet him somewhere north of the river, but in any event he would not challenge Cornwallis by marching directly across his front toward Greene's position at Cheraw.

The route of retreat was northwesterly from Broad River, and by dusk of the first day's march they reached Gilbert Town, in North Carolina. The prisoners made things difficult for the smaller column; they thought Cornwallis was on his way to their rescue and dragged their feet, pleading lameness and illness to impede the march. The guards used bayonets and, according to a witness, "drove the prisoners along like brute beasts."

The weather was cold and rainy, but there was no halt; the rutted road froze by night and was a muck at midday. The men were poorly clothed and had little food, and were nearing exhaustion when, on Jan. 23, Morgan's main body crossed the Catawba at Sherrill's Ford, despite the flood of icy waters, and went into camp on the northern bank.

Morgan had marched more than 100 miles in less than five days, across two large rivers and numerous creeks which threaded the foothills on the Carolina frontier. Soon after the main body settled in camp, William Washington arrived with his prisoners, and twenty-five more British stragglers he had caught on the way.

Morgan now began to lose men. The short enlistment period of Triplett's Virginia militia had expired, and the troops wanted to go home. Morgan sent them on—but he put the prisoners under their guard as they went northward from the Catawba toward the town of Salisbury, North Carolina. When he wrote of this move to Greene, Morgan said he had sent the British under "guard of militia whose terms expire this day—if they should go any further, militia should have the trouble of them, as they have not undergone the same fatigue as other men."

Morgan's own condition was more serious than that of his army. For several days his rheumatism, or sciatica, had pained him so keenly that he was searching for a carriage or buggy in the Catawba Valley so that he could ride northward in more comfort. The almost endless downpour of rain increased his misery, and on Jan. 23, as soon as he had dismounted in camp, he wrote Greene in despair:

> My detachment is much weakened by this fight with Tarleton. I expect we have near fifty men disabled. We have nothing to drink. . . .
> I am at this moment informed that Cornwallis is . . . on march this way, destroying everything before them. . . . I am sending off my wagons. My numbers are too weak to fight them. . . . I will do everything in my power, but you may not put too much dependence in me, for I can neither ride nor walk. . . .
> After my late success and my sanguine expectations to do something clever in this campaign I must inform you I shall be obliged to give over the pursuit by reason of an old pain returning. It is a sciatic pain in my hip that renders me

entirely incapable of active service. . . . Have had it these three weeks past, but in getting wet the other day, it has affected me more violently which gives me great pain. When I ride it takes me quick as if I were shot. . . . I am so well acquainted with this disorder that I am convinced nothing will help me but rest. . . . If I can procure a chaise I will endeavor to get home.

He suggested that other officers of the area would handle the militia as well as he, and named Generals William Davidson and Thomas Sumter and Colonel Pickens. Morgan asked for a leave until spring, saying that a winter's campaign would finish his fighting career. A few days later he reported to Greene that he was "forced to lie in a farmhouse because of rheumatism."

On the same day he sent Greene another note, his handwriting distorted as if scrawled out under intense pain. This dispatch suggested a foray into Georgia, a move Morgan had suggested some weeks earlier; he said he was willing to lead this expedition himself "but can't. I grow worse every hour and can't ride out of a walk. I am exceedingly sorry to have to leave the field at such a time as this, but it must be the case."

Morgan spent a good deal of this day writing letters, all revealing his mood of despair, just five days after conquering Tarleton. There was a flash of his fighting spirit as he wrote an old friend, William Snickers: "When you left me you remember that I was desirous to have a stroke at Tarleton—my wishes are gratified and have given him a devil of a whipping, a more complete victory was never obtained . . . entirely broke up Tarleton's Legion . . . a great thing indeed." He described his ailment and the condition of the army facing Cornwallis, but said finally: "If nobody else will fight him, I'll fight him myself."

Morgan despaired over the continual loss of the militia units, whose men went home to protect their families and tend their livestock and fields almost at will. Morgan wrote Governor Thomas Jefferson: "Great God, what is the reason we can't have more men in the field. . . . How distressing it must be to an anxious mind to see the country over-run and destroyed for want of assistance."

But even as he wrote of his troubles, Morgan saw to it that his men guarded the half-dozen fords of the Catawba near his position, and worked to build barricades which might halt or slow the British pursuit.

The Chase Begins

THE INCREDIBLE NEWS FROM COWPENS SPREAD THROUGH the country as swiftly as express riders could travel. It was Jan. 23, the day Morgan reached the Catawba, before Nathanael Greene got the word in his camp on the Pee Dee River. The five-day-old triumph was celebrated jubilantly:

A shortage of gunpowder forbade a full salute by the big guns, but as the veteran Maryland officer Col. Otho Williams wrote his friend Morgan:

> We have had a *feu de joie*, drunk all your healths [in cherry bounce, a native brandy], swore you were the finest fellows on earth, and love you, if possible, more than ever. . . . I am much better pleased that you have plucked the laurels from the brow of the hitherto fortunate Tarleton, than if he had fallen at the hands of Lucifer.

There was elation even in Greene's rather cautious report to George Washington: "The event is glorious. . . . The brilliancy and success with which it was fought does the highest honor to the American arms and adds splendor to the character of the general and his officers."

Washington told the northern army of the news in general orders, adding a touch of prophecy: "This victory, so decisive and glorious, gained with an inferior force over a select corps of British troops, reflects the highest honor on our arms and must have an important influence on the affairs of the South."

The hard-pressed rider, Major Giles, had taken the news from Richmond on to Philadelphia. The city was stirred. Congressman John Mathews, who had been made chairman of a committee to correspond with the southern army, wrote Greene:

> The intelligence received was a most healing cordial to our drooping spirits. It was so very unexpected. It seems to have had a very sensible effect on some folks, for this is convincing proof that something is to be done, in that department.

A North Carolinian in the city wrote home the opinion of military men around Congress that the battle was one of the "most well conducted actions of the war." And Abigail Adams wrote her friend Mercy Warren: "General Morgan by his repeated successes has brightened the pages of our history, and immortalized his own name . . . he is the rising Hero in the South."

John Marshall said: "Seldom had a battle, in which greater numbers were not engaged, been so important in its consequences," and the historian William Gordon predicted: "Morgan's success will be more important in its distant consequences than on the day of victory."

Congressman Ezekiel Cornell wrote Governor Greene of Rhode Island that in his opinion it was only news of Cowpens which had led Maryland to sign the Articles of Confederation and come into the fold of the United States.

Congress took action. There was little or no money, but

a gold medal was ordered struck for Morgan, and silver ones for John Eager Howard and William Washington. A sword was ordered for Andrew Pickens, and the entire little back-woods army was offered "the thanks of the United States in Congress assembled." It was to be ten years before Morgan finally got his medal.

The Virginia House of Delegates voted a fully equipped horse and a commemorative dress sword for Morgan. The governor of occupied South Carolina, John Rutledge, could do no more than send his thanks and suggest that Morgan might now conduct an offensive deep into his State and free it of British outposts, like those behind the forts at Ninety Six.

Governor Jefferson was told by an influential friend, Meriwether Smith: "I suspect that General Greene would have found himself shortly in a very perilous position" without the victory at Cowpens.

When news reached England, *The Gentleman's Magazine* took it lightly: "There is no great reason to believe our loss so great as the enemy would insinuate," but the Whig leader Horace Walpole said: "America is once more not quite ready to be conquered, although every now and then we fancy it is. Tarleton is defeated, Lord Cornwallis is checked and Arnold not sure of having betrayed his friends to much purpose."

Cowpens turned the tide against the Tories in the Carolina backwoods, which had been torn by civil war for more than ten years; eventually hundreds of men were brought back into American ranks by the victory. It soon attained the status of folklore in a ballad:

> How brave General Morgan did Tarleton defeat
> For all his proud boasting, he was forced to fly
> When brave General Morgan his courage did try
> So listen awhile and the truth I'll relate. . . .

Cornwallis wrote Lord Germain in London: "The unfortunate affair of the 17th of January was a very unexpected and severe blow."

Tarleton had by now become anxious for his reputation and asked Cornwallis to absolve him of blame for Cowpens, in writing, or to call a court-martial to investigate the affair. Cornwallis responded:

> You have forfeited no part of my esteem as an officer by the unfortunate action of the 17th: The means you used to bring the enemy to action were able and masterly, and must ever do you honor. Your disposition was unexceptionable; the total misbehavior of the troops could alone have deprived you of the glory which was so justly your due.

But Lt. Roderick Mackenzie, of the Seventy-first Highland Regiment, a critic of Tarleton, wrote the defeated cavalryman: "You got yourself and party completely ambuscaded and completely surrounded on both sides. . . . Mr. Morgan, I must say, though an enemy, showed great masterly abilities in this maneuver."

Two days after Greene received the victory dispatch from Morgan—Jan. 25—he learned that the hero of Cowpens had crossed the Catawba and halted. This move so impressed Greene that he wrote George Washington: "General Morgan . . . has very judiciously made forced marches up the country and happily crossed the Catawba."

Greene did not now know the position of Cornwallis, but assumed that the British were in pursuit of Morgan. Greene made plans to join the retreating conqueror, but first spent two hectic days preparing the main army to move.

Nathanael Greene was a fighting Quaker from Rhode Island, a plump, full-faced man of thirty-nine, a bit florid, with a full, sensual mouth. He had a cool, diffident air and a blemish in one eye from a bout with smallpox; he walked with a slight limp, the result of a boyhood injury. His backwoods troops noted that he carried a book in his pocket and read at every opportunity; the name of the author, Jonathan Swift, meant nothing to men in the ranks. The commander was also given to taking tea for refreshment. The men had been quick to see, however, that the newcomer knew his business and that their affairs might improve under him.

Greene had been read out of his Quaker Meeting when he refused to give up his place in the Home Guard of Rhode Island; as a member of the State's Assembly, he had voted for an army of defense, which he entered as a private and rose to command.

His boyhood had been spent in a rigid Quaker pattern which might have been formed in the family's ironworks; the father was a Quaker preacher and ironworker who denied worldly books to his children and for years resisted his wife's pleading to hire a tutor for them. Nathanael stole away from home to attend dances and almost as clandestinely haunted a Newport bookstore, where he was introduced to the world of letters. According to the tale they told of him in New England, the boy went timidly into the shop: "I'd like to buy a book."

"What book would you like?"

"Why, I don't know. Books. . . ."

A customer, an older man, held out a book to Nathanael and began to talk of writers and their work. They talked for a long time. The man was the Reverend Ezra Stiles, who became president of Yale. Nathanael had read hungrily, and by reading trained himself in the law; he also read widely in the classics and, when trouble came with England, trained himself as a soldier, too. He read military texts, including Saxe and Turenne, the best of them.

He had become a general in Washington's army at the siege of Boston and had displayed rare common sense. He had become Washington's intimate and had planned and built the forts which had withstood the British at the battle of Long Island. He had led the assault troops at Trenton and commanded a corps at Germantown and Monmouth. He had endured public slander in the difficult post of commissary general, in an effort to feed and clothe the desperate Continentals; he had presided over the court-martial which condemned Maj. John André in the affair of Benedict Arnold.

Long ago, when the south was threatened with invasion, Washington intended to send Greene to save the country, but Congress had insisted upon the popular hero of Saratoga, Horatio Gates. At last, late in 1780, when one American army had been lost in the siege of Charleston and Gates had lost another at Camden, Washington had summoned Greene.

The Quaker wrote his young wife: "My dear Angel, what I have been dreading has come to pass. His Excellency General Washington by order of Congress has appointed me to the command of the Southern army." He went southward without a final reunion with his wife.

Except for the guerrilla bands of Francis Marion and Thomas Sumter and a few parties in the backwoods, there was little resistance to the 8,000 British troops in Georgia and the Carolinas. In October, 1780, there was cheering news of an American victory at Kings Mountain—but there seemed no serious challenge to enemy conquest.

Greene rode south like a beggar. In Philadelphia he besieged Congress for supplies but got not even promises; there was too little money for uniforms for such an army, and credit could not be had. Merchants of the city could not help. He got the promise of 140 wagons from the Pennsylvania farm country, and of 1,000 muskets from the Continental army.

Greene rode south from Philadelphia with 180,000 dollars, Continental, in his saddlebags—almost worthless paper with which he must pay the expenses of travel for his tiny band. The party was made up of Greene, Baron von Steuben, and half a dozen aides. It paused in every State to plead for help.

In a tavern at the Head of the Elk, in Maryland, Greene ordered the local quartermaster, Daniel Yeates, to fill the State's five regular regiments and to send wagons, artisans, and money for Greene's spy system. In Annapolis, the Quaker general asked the State legislature for these things, but he reported to Washington, "They are candid enough to tell me that I must place but little dependence upon them, as they have neither money nor credit, and from the temper of the people are afraid to push matters to extremity."

Greene wrote to Caesar Rodney, the governor of Delaware, with the same pleas. He then visited Martha Washington at Mount Vernon and went down to Richmond, where he conferred with the red-haired backwoods statesman, Governor Thomas Jefferson. He asked Jefferson for 10,000 barrels of flour, 5,000 barrels of beef, 200 hogsheads of rum, 3,000 cattle, and other supplies. He gave to every influential Virginian he met the same warning: Help us now, or the British will invade and overrun your State. You will lose everything. He left with the impression that Jefferson, though sympathetic, was more interested in the theoretical rights of the people than in their freedom from the British military power. Greene spoke to the Virginia Assembly, and was applauded—but before he left, he found that intensive efforts to commandeer horses in the Virginia counties had brought in only eighteen wagon teams. Friends advised him that it was hopeless to try and raise supplies in the stricken south, but Greene did not relax his efforts; every spare moment was spent in writing to men up and down the country, urging them to send help to the southern army.

He did not conceal his concern over the future of the country from George Washington:

It has been my opinion for a long time that personal influence must supply the defects of civil constitution, but I have never been so fully convinced of it as on this journey. I believe the views and wishes of the great body of the people are entirely with us. But remove the personal influence of a few and they are a lifeless, inanimate mass, without direction or spirit to employ the means they possess for their own security.

Greene left von Steuben behind in Virginia, where he was to gather men and supplies for the southern army, and set off on horseback through the vast hardwood forests of Piedmont North Carolina. His first glimpse of the country gave him new respect for the problems of making war there: The chief settlements of the State lay to the west of a broad band of pineland in the coastal areas, and through them led the only convenient north-south trails. This must be the route of British invasion toward Virginia. The barriers were the several broad, swift rivers with their rare fords and strong currents.

Greene began work with some talented new staff officers. He had found in Richmond an unemployed artilleryman, Lt.

Col. Edward Carrington, and made him his quartermaster. Carrington's first assignment was to study the Dan River, which lay between North Carolina and Virginia; if it were navigable deep into the upcountry, supplies might be brought up. Boats were to be collected, and fords marked for future use.

At Hillsboro, the village capital of North Carolina, Greene found that both the army of Gates and the State's government had fled. Greene wrote to State officials for aid and also found an able engineer for his army, the Polish émigré, Col. Thaddeus Kosciusko. He sent the Pole to study the Catawba River, and Brig. Gen. Edward Stevens, a leader of Virginia militia, to study the Yadkin River. Thus, before he had seen his new army or located the position of his enemy, Greene had scouted the country over which he must march and fight, and prepared to deal with its river barriers.

Greene found his army in the village of Charlotte, North Carolina, near the South Carolina border. He managed a cordial greeting with Gates, whom he relieved without the formality of a court of inquiry; Gates went home to Virginia. Greene arrived on Dec. 2, 1780. He stayed up all that night, pressing his shrewd questions upon Col. Thomas Polk, the Commissary General under Gates. For hours he probed the state of the army, military supply and conditions of the countryside, the strength of the enemy. Polk told his friends: "By morning, he understood the situation better than Gates had in his whole time with the army."

Greene's men watched him with care, but most of them were deceived by the look of reserve on the calm face, which Light-Horse Harry Lee thought "a goodness which seemed to shade and soften the fire and greatness."

Orders of Dec. 3 announced the change in command.

Greene was surprised to find that there was almost no ammunition, that there was only a three days' supply of provisions, and none in prospect from the country, which had been picked clean by foragers. He found that there was not a scrap of a record for the army, no accounts of its arms, ammunition, funds, contributions of States, terms of troops, commissions awarded—nothing. Greene at once began putting things in order:

Kosciusko was sent down the Pee Dee River in South Carolina to find a neighborhood where the army might camp and draw upon plantations not yet plundered. Carrington was sent to Richmond for supplies, including tools, a ton of nails, and shipwrights to build flatboats, which would be carried on wagons. He ordered a prison camp built at Salisbury, with a hospital nearby directed by Dr. William Read, an experienced army surgeon. From a mine in southwest Virginia, at Chiswell's, he ordered lead shipped to the North Carolina Moravian towns on the upper Yadkin, where cartridges would be made. His foragers came upon a supply of denim and sheeting, which Greene sent to Salisbury, where women of the town made shirts and overalls for the troops—these women were to be paid in precious salt, hauled in army wagons from the coast. From Hunter's Ironworks at Fredericksburg, Virginia, he ordered 1,500 pounds of bar iron, for horseshoes and other essentials. He ordered that supply magazines be built on the Catawba and Yadkin.

To the North Carolina Board of War, a timid and inefficient body, Greene wrote that he must have supplies for the army or abandon the State to the enemy, adding that the State must "begin by providing for the belly for that is the main spring of every operation."

Greene made his first speech to the troops and saw their

miserable condition. He wrote North Carolina's Governor Abner Nash that he had "but the shadow of an army in the midst of distress."

He was more explicit in writing to Lafayette: ". . . a few ragged, half-starving troops in the wilderness, destitute of everything necessary for either the comfort or convenience of soldiers . . . the country is almost laid waste and the inhabitants plunder one another with little less than savage fury. We live from hand to mouth." He advised the young Frenchman not to join him in the southern adventure.

To Thomas Sumter: "It is a great misfortune that the little force we have is in such a wretched state for want of clothing. More than half our numbers are in a manner naked, so much so that we cannot put them on the least kind of duty. Indeed, there is a great number that have not a rag of clothes on them except a little piece of blanket, in the Indian form around their waists."

Men deserted every night, and there was no way to count them in their comings and goings. Greene circulated a rumor to the effect that deserters would be shot, but the tide did not dwindle. When Greene caught his first deserter, he had the man tried and condemned and drew up the army to witness the work of the firing squad. He sent officers among the men at night to learn their reaction and got one laconic comment from a private at a campfire: "It is new Lords, new laws." Desertion became rare.

Greene sent home two units of Virginia dragoons because they had too little clothing to take the field. He wrote Jefferson: "No man will think himself bound to fight the battle of a State that leaves him to perish for want of covering."

First returns gave Greene an army of 2,307 men, on

paper; more than half of these were short-term militia, only 800 of the total equipped and fit for fighting. Thus Greene began, without a cent to pay for even such expenses as the letters he continually sent through the country, or to buy intelligence reports. He and his officers had to live in free quarters, or those commandeered from householders.

Colonel Otho Williams of Maryland became his adjutant general. To aid Carrington, Greene persuaded a guerrilla cavalry leader, Col. William R. Davie, to become commissary general of purchases—to find food and war supplies in the area. Davie refused at first, saying that he knew nothing of money or accounts. Greene replied that he would not be troubled with such matters, since there was not a penny in the treasury. Davie accepted the post and became an efficient "purveyor of beef and bacon, an inspector of invoices, a contractor for salt and tobacco . . . gathering herds of swine and bargaining for barrels of rum."

In the midst of plans Greene had bad news from the north: He could no longer expect the 1,000 promised muskets, since a shipment from France was delayed; there would be no more money—and there was a report that the British would launch a major offensive in the south in the coming spring in an effort to end the war.

Greene called a council of war with his senior officers and made a proposal that astonished them—an attack on Cornwallis in his camp at Winnsboro, South Carolina. The commander reluctantly followed the advice of the council and abandoned the plan; he agreed' to move more slowly. When Kosciusko returned from the Cheraw country with a glowing report, Greene determined to leave Charlotte. It was his first, and perhaps most important, strategic decision.

He split his tiny army in two, taking the main body southward to Cheraw and sending Daniel Morgan into western South Carolina. His orders to the Old Wagoner were clear:

> . . . This force . . . you will employ against the enemy either offensively or defensively as your own prudence and discretion may direct. . . . The object of this detachment is to give protection to that part of the country and spirit up the people.

The two armies moved from Charlotte on Dec. 20, the first day that a series of heavy rains permitted them to take the road; Greene required six days to move his force the eighty miles to Cheraw. Morgan had disappeared in the foothills of the frontier. Greene had every confidence in the Old Wagoner; he knew him as a superb leader of troops—but since he had no faith in the militia, he expected nothing so stunning as a victory over Tarleton. His dispatches to Morgan during their time of separation reflected Greene's anxiety. The commander spent his own time during that month in an effort to persuade North Carolina to raise regular troops and abandon the militia system.

He urged the State's Board of War to give him regulars and was refused. The Board called out one class of militia, and Greene declined to make use of it. Just a week before Morgan's militia won their victory by standing firm with the regulars at Cowpens, Greene wrote of "shoals of useless militia, who, like the locusts of Egypt, have eaten up everything, and the expense has been so enormous that it has ruined the currency of the state. . . . I am persuaded North Carolina had militia enough to swallow up all the revenues of America, especially under their imperfect arrangements, where every man draws and wastes as much as he pleases."

Despite everything, Greene had brought some order to his little army at Cheraw. A trickle of supplies now came from von Steuben in Virginia, though Greene was forced to issue stern orders that officers in his outposts should not seize these supplies when wagons passed them, whatever their needs —and especially must they keep their hands off the rum.

Smallpox appeared in camp, and there were serious cases of malnutrition; more doctors were gathered to set up a crude hospital and treat the men. The refugee Governor John Rutledge hung around camp and, as nominal commander of the South Carolina militia, demanded much of Greene's attention.

There were squabbles among the official family: General Smallwood's vanity provoked a quarrel, and he went home to Maryland. Greene corresponded frequently with the back-country guerrillas, especially Francis Marion and Thomas Sumter, and conducted a correspondence of diplomacy when Sumter was offended by Morgan's intrusion into his district. The quarrel grew so warm that Sumter directed his officers to disregard all orders from Morgan, unless approved by the Sumter signature.

The last important arrival in the camp on the Pee Dee was Harry Lee, lately promoted to lieutenant colonel after a distinguished career of derring-do in the northern campaigns. Lee came belatedly on Jan. 9, with about 280 men in his green-clad cavalry Legion. Lee had long waited in Philadelphia, refusing to move until Congress provided money for travel. He had recruited 25 men in Richmond on the way south—and when he reached South Carolina was promised 150 more by Governor Rutledge.

Greene could not feed the Legion in this camp and sent it over the river to help Francis Marion and his predatory band in the coastal South Carolina swamps.

Greene was not slow to recognize the value of Light-Horse Harry Lee, a handsome, vain, and ambitious soldier who was not yet twenty-five years old. The cavalryman came from one of Virginia's most influential families; his forebears had helped to rule the colony since 1600, when the first of the American Lees arrived from England. There was a rich military heritage in the clan which ran back to the time of William the Conqueror and through the Crusades and most of England's bloody wars.

Henry Lee had been trained at the College of New Jersey at Princeton and when war came was ready to study law in England; he entered the army as a cavalry captain and after Brandywine and Germantown was one of Washington's favorite officers, trusted with the cavalry screen protecting the army. The British, stung by his frequent raids on their communications and supply lines, made many vain attempts to eliminate Harry and his Virginia Horse.

Three years before, in one of the sensational exploits of the war, Lee and seven companions, trapped in the Spread Eagle Tavern near Valley Forge, had resisted so fiercely as to drive off 200 British horsemen who had surrounded the place. It was Lee who had laid the plans for the capture of the traitor Benedict Arnold; these had failed, but Lee soon won new fame by leading a surprise assault on a British fort at Paulus Hook, New Jersey, with 300 men, gaining entrance by dressing ten of his soldiers as peddlers of produce and taking the garrison.

Lee's Legion of light troops, mixed infantry and cavalry, were reputed as "the finest troops" to appear in the war, the American counterpart of the feared Legion of Tarleton, inspired by a commander described as having "come from his mother's womb a soldier." Lee had spent most of his inheritance, a considerable fortune, in raising, equipping, and feeding this small force of rebellion.

In the future his oratory would capture the country's imagination as he eulogized Washington as "First in war, first in peace. . . ." He would also become the father of an even more famous soldier, Robert E. Lee.

Harry Lee and Francis Marion were ideal companions in the hit-and-run warfare of the South Carolina marshes, and in the hideaway of the Swamp Fox they planned a daring raid. Their target was the small port of Georgetown, on Winyah Bay at the mouth of the Pee Dee River, where a British garrison of 200 manned a fort. The partisan officers asked Greene's consent for the assault.

The general was dubious. A victory would open the Pee Dee to supply boats for the army and give Cornwallis pause in his drive into North Carolina. On the other hand, the little army could not afford the loss of either corps of raiders, and if they were trapped in the village, Greene might need all his men for a rescue attempt. In brief, the success of the unfolding campaign was at stake, and Greene urged caution upon Lee: "Get good information before you attempt anything." He then gave grudging consent to the assault.

The thrust against Georgetown served only to warn the British that their outposts were vulnerable to raids. The attack became something of a comedy. Spies had reported that the enemy troops slept outside the tiny fort in barracks and might be surprised by night. The American infantry was loaded in flatboats and floated down the river, where the men were hidden on an island above Georgetown for one day. Twenty-four hours after this move began the cavalry took the overland route, Lee and Marion waiting in the woodlands outside town until 2 A.M., when the infantry was to strike.

The foot soldiers entered the town on schedule, were posted between the barracks and the fort, and the British commander, a Lieutenant Colonel Campbell, was taken prisoner. A few shots fired as Campbell's quarters were forced brought in the American horsemen—to no avail. The British soldiers calmly barricaded themselves in the barracks, and since the fort was still held by the enemy, Lee and Marion realized that dawn would bring them under a severe cross fire. They released Campbell on parole, and the town was left to the British. There were no casualties.

A few days after their return to Marion's camp there was news of the victory at Cowpens. Greene ordered them to round up horses for cavalry and wagon teams in the Pee Dee country; they would be needed for the retreat which was sure to come. Greene advised them that he would go to Charlotte for a conference with General Morgan and the militia leaders, William Davidson, Andrew Pickens, and Thomas Sumter.

There was an immediate change of plan, for news of Morgan's retreat and pursuit by Cornwallis canceled the conference. The scene of action had now shifted to the Catawba. Greene advised Lee that he had gone to join Morgan and that the Legion should come to the main army as quickly as possible. He also took care to prepare the way in the rear. He ordered boats made ready on the distant Dan River, in Virginia, asked von Steuben to send more troops, and urged frontier militia commanders to come out.

Greene ordered Marion to operate in the rear of Cornwallis. The prisoners were sent north under General Stevens and his departing Virginians, bound for Charlottesville; Greene advised Governor Jefferson to expect them. Stevens was told to keep supply officers a day ahead of the column of prisoners to gather food for a quick march. He urged North Carolina officials to raise troops and to send £1,000 for needs of the army. He wrote to Congressmen, including John Mathews, warning that within a few weeks he might be forced to disband the army: "Our prospects are gloomy notwithstanding these flashes of success."

On Jan. 28 Greene turned over the main army to Brig. Gen. Isaac Huger of South Carolina with orders to march it northward toward Salisbury, North Carolina, where it might unite with Morgan. He then set out on horseback over the Tory-infested country with an aide, a guide, and a sergeant's guard of cavalry. His goal was Morgan's camp on the Catawba, more than 125 miles away. The long race was on.

Greene was a little more than two days on his ride. The main army moved behind him on Jan. 29 in two brigades, the Virginians under Huger and the Maryland and Delaware troops under Otho Williams. The army made forced marches for 150 miles to the north in the cold, rainy weather, without tents, ill-clad, and with little food or drink. There were no desertions in this time.

From the Catawba Greene wrote Huger in detail, citing the position of the enemy and plans for the retreat: "I wish to avoid action until our force is collected. It is necessary we should take every possible precaution to guard against a misfortune. But I am not without hopes of ruining Lord Cornwallis, if he persists in his mad scheme of pushing through the country. . . . Here is a fine field and great glory ahead."

Charles Cornwallis was already, at forty-two, a distinguished figure in the British Army, a veteran of long wars against the French and Saxons. He had fought at the siege of Cassel, and on the Oder, at Paderborn, Wilhelmstadt, and

Kirch Donkern. He had been schooled at Eton, where he got a cocked eye on the hockey field, and was trained for war at the Turin Academy. He was the second Earl Cornwallis and the first Marquis. An uncle was the Archbishop of Canterbury, and Cornwallis himself had been a favorite of George III, a Lord of the Bedchamber, Constable of the Tower, Vice-treasurer of Ireland. One ancestor had been High Sheriff of London in 1378.

Despite everything, he had sided with the Whigs on the colonial question; he was opposed to the American war but when he was ordered to duty overseas went more willingly than many British troops—some of whom mutinied at the docks. He fought well in northern campaigns, commanding corps at Germantown and Brandywine, but he lost his Hessians at Trenton and gave futile chase to Washington in New Jersey.

The Earl had been called home upon the illness of his wife in 1778 and after her death had been more reluctant than ever to return to war against the rebellious colonists. It was not only the loss of his lovely Jemima Tullikens which depressed Cornwallis, for he told friends in England of America: "I never saw a stronger country, or one better calculated for the defensive."

In the south, when he was left by Sir Henry Clinton to face the rebel army, Cornwallis lost some of his assurance. He wrote complaints to London of the winter cold, the gales and the rutted roads, the creeks which were in fact rivers, the inconstant native Tories, the ferocious Whigs. He made it clear to Henry Clinton that the American army placed him at a disadvantage: "They always keep at a considerable distance, and retire on our approach. But the constant incursions of refugees, North Carolinians, back mountain men, and the perpetual rising in different parts of this province . . . keep the whole country in continual alarm, and render the assistance of regular troops everywhere necessary."

The ghostly armies of American guerrillas were threatening enough; one band ended his first invasion of North Carolina at Kings Mountain; others still ambushed his foragers each time they left the security of his picket lines. There were also uncertainties of command. Neither Lord Germain in London nor Clinton in New York seemed to understand the perils of launching an offensive across the hostile Carolina wilderness against superior numbers—all without supply bases or lines of communication or the prospect of reinforcement.

Cornwallis did his best: He empowered his officers as civil magistrates, who plundered the people of South Carolina despite efforts to control them. He executed deserters in public hangings and jailed many others, for he believed in war without quarter, once the issue was drawn:

> All the inhabitants of this province . . . who have taken part in this revolt, should be punished with the greatest rigor, that they should be imprisoned, and their whole property taken from them or destroyed. . . . I have ordered in the most positive manner, that every militia man who had borne arms with us and afterwards joined the enemy should be immediately hanged.

The British had hanged some Georgia militiamen captured after a skirmish, and in retaliation many of those captured from the British force at Kings Mountain had been hanged. Cornwallis and Greene carried on a correspondence about these barbarities, to no avail. The civil war raged beyond the control of commanders, though from afar Cornwallis appeared in the role of executioner. The English Whig William Fitzpatrick wrote Benjamin Franklin: "Lord Cornwallis' . . . cool butcheries of defenseless people in South Carolina irrevocably seals the perpetual disunion between Great Britain and America." And Horace Walpole said: "The conqueror talks of severity to the late renegades; he forgets his own protests to the Stamp Act, or perhaps chooses to wash it out with blood."

But within Cornwallis's army, as it lay in camp at Winnsboro, South Carolina, early in 1781, young officers saw the commander as a hero: "There is no man more likely or deserving than Lord Cornwallis," one of them wrote. "His army is a family, he is the father of it. There are no parties, no competitions."

Nathanael Greene had an appreciation for Cornwallis and once wrote Anthony Wayne: "Be a little careful, and tread softly; for, depend upon it, you have a modern Hannibal to deal with in the person of Cornwallis."

The Earl prepared to open his offensive with about 3,500 men—though Clinton estimated the strength at 4,000. In mid-December, 1780, reinforcements landed at Charleston under General Leslie. The newcomers were doubly welcome, for they included the Brigade of Guards, a crack regiment of the British Army, every man a fine physical specimen of 6 feet or more. There was also a good German regiment, the Bose, and a detachment of the best of the German professionals—the Yagers, riflemen who had volunteered for the service, all expert hunters and soldiers who commanded high pay and superior clothing. There was also a detachment of dragoons. The new force under Leslie was ordered to bring these units to Cornwallis, a reinforcement of 1,530 men.

Leslie was slow to move, for he had lost draft horses on the rough voyage from Virginia aboard small boats. It was only on his fifth day in Charleston that he marched inland, and as he passed the swamps he was harassed by guerrilla marksmen. The new force was twelve days in moving to Camden, where it was ordered to camp.

Cornwallis gathered supplies and ordered Banastre Tarleton to scout the roads to the north, saying: "The friends hereabouts are so timid, and so stupid, that I can get no intelligence." To guard his flanks from the mountain men, the Earl sent officers to incite the Cherokees to raid the western North Carolina settlements, on the ground that they were encroachments on Indian territory. Many mountaineers soon left Greene and Morgan to defend their homes. Though fresh atrocities were reported on the frontier, Cornwallis defended his Indian allies: "Their humanity is in striking contrast to the shocking barbarities committed by the mountaineers."

The British commander also sent a party of 400 men up the coast to secure the port of Wilmington, open the Cape Fear River, and protect the right flank of the army as it advanced. When he felt that he was ready to move, Cornwallis called Leslie's troops to him but realized that he would need Tory aid as well:

We will give our friends in North Carolina a fair trial. If they behave like men, it may be of the greatest advantage to Britain. If they are as dastardly and pusillanimous as our friends to the southward, we must leave them to their fate, and secure what we have got.

Thus, on the first day of 1781, Cornwallis opened the game. He sent Tarleton and some 1,100 men west to deal with Morgan and with his main force moved leisurely northward, his first march on Jan. 7, with Leslie trailing in the rear, now held up by heavy wagons at the fords of swollen streams. By Jan. 17 the big army had moved only thirty miles, to Turkey Creek, a point some twenty-five miles east of Kings Mountain, from which Cornwallis hoped to intercept Morgan in the event of his retreat.

A handful of Tarleton's fleeing dragoons rode into the camp on the night of Jan. 17 with tales of disaster; the commander was anxious, but he could not ascertain the full extent of the defeat. The next morning, when about two hundred of the survivors of Cowpens had come in, Tarleton arrived with his report. An American prisoner of war saw the scene: Cornwallis was leaning forward on his sword as the cavalryman told of his defeat and the capture of most of his men. The Earl became so angry that he pressed down on the sword until it snapped and swore in a loud voice that he would recapture the prisoners from Morgan, whatever the cost.

Still Cornwallis did not move. Leslie was a day's march behind, and the army waited for him. The orders of the day called for three days' rations and one day's issue of rum to be given the troops. It was dawn of Jan. 19 before the long column trailed into the road northward in chase of Morgan. The German Yagers led the way, with the hospital train, a herd of cattle, and droves of women and freed Negroes in the rear.

Tarleton rode off with the reorganized remnant of his army and a few other troops in an effort to find Morgan and, if possible, to set free the prisoners. After two days Tarleton found the Americans far beyond his reach and he returned to Cornwallis.

The main army wallowed along on the wrong road for two days then turned toward the east, after crossing into North Carolina on the second day. It reached Tryon Courthouse on Jan. 23 and at last came to the settlement of Ramsour's Mill. The orders of the day reflected the Earl's growing concern that the swift Americans would escape him:

The commanding officers of the different corps will examine the best communications with those on the right, that there may be no delay or improper interval when the line is ordered to march.

Any officer who shall observe a break in the line of march, will send forward to acquaint Lord Cornwallis . . . and not pass the word to halt as has been sometimes practiced. . . .

The women of the different corps are to remain behind with the baggage guards.

Cornwallis remained at Ramsour's Mill for two days, busy with supplying shoes and extra soles to his troops, enforcing orders limiting officers in their ownership of both Negroes and horses ("No woman or Negro to possess a horse"), and in reading to the men a letter of congratulations from London upon the victory of Camden the past August. Only then did he order the army to burn most of the baggage wagons and huge quantities of the stores gathered in South Carolina. The Earl set an example by tossing into the flames much of his own personal equipment.

By Jan. 28, when Cornwallis finally marched, Morgan had carried his prisoners in a fifty-mile circle around the British army, never more than twenty-five miles distant.

The British, finding that Morgan's route lay to the northeast, turned toward the Catawba fords. Cornwallis now commanded light troops, in effect, since of his remaining wagons four were reserved for the sick and wounded and the rest bore medicines, salt, and ammunition. All the supplies needed for a long, hard campaign had gone up in the thick smoke at Ramsour's Mill. As he marched in the last days of January, the river rose ahead of Cornwallis, filling with violent rains. A two-day issue of rum was given out, and the rest of the supply was poured on the ground. The Earl reported that

"There was the most general and cheerful acquiescence" to this destruction by his troops, but Americans of the region were soon welcoming numbers of British and Hessian deserters—by some counts a total of 250 men. At the end of the first month of marching, the army's returns showed a loss of 227 British troops not accounted for as battle casualties; the Brigade of Guards had dwindled by an eighth.

Cornwallis promised the remaining troops only hardship:

> Lord Cornwallis has so often experienced the zeal and good will of the troops, that he has not the smallest doubt that the officers and soldiers will most cheerfully submit to the inconveniences which must naturally attend a war so remote from water-carriages and the magazines of the army. The supply of rum for a time will be absolutely impossible, and that of meal very uncertain. To remedy the latter, it is recommended either to bruise the Indian corn, or to rasp it after it has been soaked.

The British column deliberately slowed its march as it drew near the Catawba, to confuse scouts as to its destination among the fords. Cornwallis arrived at Beattie's Ford on the afternoon of Jan. 28, concluded that the river was too high to cross, and fell back four miles to the plantation of Jacob Forney; he sent patrols to gather information about the American position.

On Jan. 29 two British soldiers who wandered a few yards from their camp were snatched by guerrillas. Cornwallis issued a warning against straggling. There was a British inspection the next day as the army lay near the river, waiting for the fall of the water in the fords. The refugee Royal governor of North Carolina, Josiah Martin, watched as Cornwallis reviewed the troops.

By the last day of January Cornwallis knew the American positions well enough to realize that further delay might be dangerous, as well as useless. The day's rainfall promised an even higher river for several days, and he determined to move. His spies told him that Greene was on the Catawba, and that the main American army was hurrying up from Cheraw to join Morgan.

A Tory guide was found, one Fred Hager, and at 1 A.M. on Feb. 1, long before the coming of the winter dawn, Cornwallis sent Negroes, women, and the sick to the rear and led his troops toward the crossing.

The British army of pursuit had spent eight days in covering less than eighty miles, many of these in the wrong direction. Later critics, British and American, would point to the burning of the baggage at Ramsour's Mill as the downfall of Cornwallis, but now, at least, he was ready for swift movement.

Cowan's Ford

THE BRAWLING CATAWBA ROSE IN THE MOUNTAINS AND, when it had emerged from the foothills after a long course eastward, veered to the south, making lazy turns toward the South Carolina border. Tangles of briar and bamboo and dense hardwood thickets screened the waterway, and the rains of the season sent the dark flood foaming among the rocks of the riverbed. Along the relatively straight north-south course of the river just to the northwest of Charlotte, Daniel Morgan had rested with his army.

Downstream from his position at Sherrill's Ford were five passages of the river in the neighborhood, in this order: McEwen's, Beattie's, Cowan's, Tool's, and Tuckasege. Some of these were little-known outside the area and were private farm crossings. Even lesser fords had been filled with stones and debris to make them impassable, under orders from Morgan.

On Jan. 29 the rheumatic commander stirred from his bed and despite intense pain rode downstream to Beattie's Ford. He had no doubt that the British could force the river; he saw their advance that day, and scouts told him that Cornwallis was only ten miles distant. But Morgan was cheered by the crowded camp at Beattie's. More than 800 men had come in with Gen. William Davidson, and they seemed to be in a fighting mood. Davidson knew his Scotch-Irish neighbors well and had lured them with a shrewd bargain: For six weeks of service he would give them three months' credit for militia service; they had come in surprising numbers. Many came as members of warlike Presbyterian congregations of the region. A messenger from Davidson had arrived at Fourth Creek Church while the Reverend James Hall was preaching, and handed his dispatch to the pastor— who halted his sermon, read the appeal, and called for volunteers to ride with him. Most of these churchmen had come under Captain Hall. Centre Church sent a party under its pastor, Thomas McCaule.

Many patriots had failed the army. Hundreds of Whig families were hiding in the deep woods, their furniture, food, and other valuables secreted in hollow trees or buried. Livestock was tied in thickets far from the farmhouses. Schools in the path of the British had been dismissed. Refugees were in the roads northward.

The hundreds who had come to Davidson were a tribute to the popularity of the brigadier who had been raised in this neighborhood, though born in Pennsylvania. He was now thirty-five years old, a veteran Indian fighter who had been wounded because of his reckless exposure in battle, a graduate of a Charlotte academy, and a soldier of experience in the northern army. He had become a militia captain at the outbreak of war and rose to command regulars, was a lieutenant colonel after Brandywine, and by the winter of Valley Forge had intimate friends in the army's officer corps, including

Light-Horse Harry Lee. Davidson had returned south with the tide of war and now commanded militia in the western district of North Carolina. His home was nearby, not far from the spot where a college would rise, bearing his name.

Morgan put his new men to work. Captured British scouts told him that Cornwallis was marching for Salisbury, and the Old Wagoner put his prisoners on the road, sending them by way of the Moravian towns on the upper Yadkin. Davidson was ordered to organize a defense of the fords; Morgan rode back to camp at Sherrill's.

Tuckasege Ford was on the road from Ramsour's to Charlotte, and Davidson placed 200 men there, Surry County militia under Col. Joseph Williams; Tool's was guarded by 70 Mecklenburg County militia; Cowan's was held by Lt. Thomas Davidson of Mecklenburg and about 25 men.

Trees were felled in the roads at Tuckasege and Tool's Fords, ditches were dug, and parapets raised.

Davidson made his headquarters at Beattie's with 500 men, including the cavalry of a young Mecklenburg captain, Joseph Graham. There were 50 of these young troopers, armed with swords from blacksmith shops, rifles and pistols, and knives. Graham's troops went over the river on Jan. 30 to sniff out the enemy and were chased back by Tarleton's dragoons. They found Cornwallis at Forney's plantation, where he had dispossessed the owner of the log house.

In the rain of Jan. 31, at 2 P.M., just as his dispatch had indicated, Nathanael Greene appeared with his mud-splashed party at Beattie's Ford. He met Morgan and William Washington, surveyed the situation for a few minutes, learned that Morgan's troops were already moving north, the prisoners in advance, and that the enemy was just across the river.

Greene then left his lieutenants and with William Davidson walked a few yards away to sit on a log; the two were in earnest conversation for some twenty minutes. No one overheard their plans. A large party of British cavalry appeared on the opposite bank of the river while Greene and Davidson talked, and an enemy officer, thought to be Cornwallis, studied the position with a field glass.

Greene's quick inspection of the fords was enough; he ordered Davidson to patrol the crossings with cavalry throughout the night, warning that Cornwallis would probably try to push cavalry over some unguarded ford in the hours of darkness, so that he could take American infantry in the rear next morning.

Greene also hurried off dispatch riders: He ordered General Huger to take the main army to Salisbury as soon as possible, sending all surplus stores north to Guilford Courthouse. He also sent a plea to Col. William Campbell, a hero of Kings Mountain, to come with 1,000 of his frontier riflemen.

Greene now hoped to make a stand with the militia on the Catawba, while Morgan joined Huger and other reinforcements at Salisbury. If that could be done, the Quaker might choose his own ground for a general engagement.

Within an hour after Greene had left him, William Davidson led Graham's cavalry and 250 infantry under Col. William Polk to Cowan's Ford, four miles below Beattie's. He left a band of 250 at Beattie's under Col. Thomas Farmer of Orange County. Davidson and Graham rode together.

"General Greene had never been on the Catawba before," Davidson said, "but he appeared to know more about it than men who've been raised here on its banks."

Graham was ordered to patrol the vicinity all night.

They reached Cowan's at dusk, and Davidson took most of his men rearward. The tiny picket at the river's edge was left alone.

Lieutenant Thomas Davidson's party, of about twenty-five or thirty men, lay quite near the water on a flat which was overgrown with cane, haw, and persimmon. Behind them, the road which emerged from the river crossing climbed a steep hill. Wilderness surrounded them.

Cowan's Ford had two crossings, their locations known only to neighbors. A horse ford ran obliquely up the river, to emerge about a quarter of a mile above Lt. Tom Davidson's picket. This crossing was smoother, shallower, and easier, despite its greater length. General Davidson, anticipating that the enemy would use that crossing, rather than the more direct and difficult wagon ford, had placed his strong force to meet them. He was also sure that British scouts must have seen the picket on the riverbank, but that his own presence had not been detected in the darkness.

The night was very dark and the stream so swift that few sounds could be heard over the powerful roar of the water. Waiting soldiers knew that horseback riders braving that current would be tumbled downstream.

The soldiers of the Cowan's picket were the greenest of militiamen, most of them boys in homemade hunting shirts and moccasins, carrying a variety of flintlock weapons; some of the bayonets were made from pitchforks. Few of these young men had heard shots fired in anger.

One of the picket was Robert Henry, sixteen, who had come to the army when he heard a rumor that Tarleton was catching Whig boys "to make musicians out of them." He bought half a pint of native whiskey for 100 dollars, Continental, borrowed a gun, and with a friend, Charles Rutledge, joined the picket at the ford.

Lieutenant Davidson welcomed the two boys: "Cornwallis will come across here tomorrow morning as sure as gun's iron—and maybe he'll come tonight. Everybody in the picket has got a stand to annoy 'em when they come into the river, and I want you to pick your stand. We don't want to be crowded when the time comes."

Rutledge picked the uppermost position and Henry the lower one, nearest the path of the wagon ford itself.

Lieutenant Davidson was all confidence as dusk came on: "They couldn't come across here with a million men, unless they had cannon—so long as our ammunition holds out. I think the General's all wrong to put most of the men up at the other ford. I hope they've got scouts over at Forney's, to let us know when they move this way."

The lieutenant then staged a drill, sending all the men to their stands with orders to examine the terrain in detail, so that they could find these spots when the time came. Robert Henry had a long memory of these moments:

"I went to mine and was well pleased with it—for in shooting, if I would miss my first aim, my lead would range along the British army obliquely and still do damage, and I could stand it until the British would come to a place where the water was riffling over a rock, then it would be time to run away."

When he had studied his position, Henry looked over the guard for familiar faces and found only two: his crippled schoolmaster, Robert Beatty, and a neighbor, Joel Jetton. Robert Henry settled with his companions to wait in the cold mist. The men huddled for warmth by their fires.

Soon after dark there was the imitation hoot of an owl

across the river; there was a reply and Henry saw a figure go down to a canoe at the water's edge and return with a report: "All quiet in the British camp."

The Cowan's picket slept with guns in hand, and at daybreak only one of them, Joel Jetton, came to life. He had somehow heard the splashing of horses in the noisy river. He ran to the ford, where he found the sentry asleep and kicked him into the river. Jetton tried to fire at the dim figures in the river, but his gun did not spark. He ran back to the fires of the picket, yelling, "The British! The British!" and fired his rifle. The picket stumbled to its feet and scattered to the assigned stands.

Robert Henry was with the last of them: "When I got to my stand I saw redcoats, but thought from loss of sleep my eyes might be mistaken, threw water into them; I then heard the British splashing and making a noise as if drowning. I fired, and continued firing until I saw that one on horseback had passed my rock in the river."

On the last day of January Cornwallis made an elaborate attempt to deceive his enemies. He marched the army at 9 A.M. an aimless route of a few miles before settling down, ostensibly for the night. His camp, however, was somewhat nearer to Cowan's than to the better-known public ford, at Beattie's. His orders of the day were more secretive than usual—though they prescribed an order of march, they divided the army into two columns, adding: "Lieut.-Col. Webster will give orders respecting the other column."

The British strategy was simple: Lt. Col. James Webster, an able young Scot, the son of a famous Edinburgh minister, would lead a large diversionary force to Beattie's Ford, fire the six-pounder cannon across the river, and alarm the defenders of all fords in the region. Webster would take the Thirty-third Regiment, a battalion of the Seventy-first, Hamilton's corps of North Carolina Tories, the Yagers, the big guns, and all the wagons. Cornwallis would lead the rest of the army in the real attack at Cowan's, cross the river, and wheel upstream to take the defenders of Beattie's in the rear— if they stood against Webster's noisy show of strength.

Cornwallis led the movement at 1 A.M., riding with native guides at the head of his column toward Cowan's. Behind him came the shock troops: Lieutenant Colonel Hall with some picked light infantry of the Guards, the Brigade of Guards, the Bose Regiment, the Twenty-third Regiment (Royal Welsh Fusileers), Tarleton's corps. There were also two smaller cannon, three-pounders.

The roads to the ford were little more than cattle trails and at one point led through a woodland where there was not so much as a track. One of the guns overturned in a swampy spot here, and the Bose Regiment and others who came behind lost their way because of a break in the column. Some of the gunners from the leading cannon stayed behind to help with the unlucky gun; one of these men had the only firing match in the attacking force.

When Cornwallis and Brigadier General O'Hara, of the Guards, reached the river with the head of the column, it was raining. They saw from the campfires over the stream that the Americans were more numerous than expected—and also found that they could not fire the cannon. Cornwallis momentarily debated whether he should postpone the attack but decided to move on, since the river would likely rise even higher during the day. Failure to fire the cannon at Cowan's gave the British a few additional minutes to approach without discovery.

O'Hara formed the Guards into columns of fours, and as the coming of dawn lightened the scene, he rode out with a Tory guide at his side, gingerly leading the first of the Guards into the swirling stream. Each of the Guards carried an empty musket slung high on the left shoulder with fixed bayonet. The men felt their way along with long staves to brace themselves in the current, but the files were soon jumbled. The bottom was rocky and rough and the footing precarious. The vanguard halted while men and officers lashed themselves together in small groups to prevent being carried away by the turbulent water.

The Guards had been ordered not to fire until they had crossed the river, and Cornwallis now saw that any musket work would have been impossible. His horse was soon chest-deep in the stream, barely able to keep his feet. Men were plunging waist-deep as soon as they left the bank, and many fell into holes and were forced to swim.

General O'Hara's horse rolled over, and the struggling pair was swept about 40 yards downstream before the officer got to his feet and led the animal toward safety. The second in command, General Leslie, was carried downriver by the current, his horse turning and twisting helplessly for several minutes.

By now the Americans had begun firing. When the signal shot of Joel Jetton sounded, the first line of British infantry was near the middle of the river. Cornwallis's horse staggered beneath him, wounded, but plodded on toward the far shore. Men were wounded in ranks, but after a brief halt the files pushed forward.

Sergeant Roger Lamb, who was near the head of the Royal Welsh Fusileers, entered the crossing about this time. He was moved with admiration for the brave troops ahead

of him: "Wading over this ford, upwards of 500 yards wide
[it was actually about 400 yards], up to their breasts in a
rapid stream, their knapsacks on their backs, 60 or 70 pounds
of powder and ball in each pouch, tied at the fold of their
necks, their firelocks with bayonets fixed on their shoulders,
300 of their enemies, accounted the best marksmen in the
world, placed on a hill as it were over their heads, keeping
a continual and very heavy fire upon them."

In truth, it was only the tiny band of Lt. Thomas Davidson which at first opposed the British, and firing was sporadic
until they were reinforced.

Sergeant Lamb reached the center of the river, hanging
tightly to a soldier beside him. Just in front of him a gunner,
a short man, lost his grip on one of the cannon which he was
trying to guide and was swept away. The water was now
over 4 feet deep and more rocky than ever. Lamb called to
his men to hold fast to each other and to press on, regardless
of firing. He then rescued the gunner:

"I knew that if this artillery man was either killed or
drowned, his loss would be great indeed, as we had no man at
hand who could supply his place in working the gun. . . . I
threw myself on my belly on the surface of the water, and in
nine or ten strong strokes, I overtook him. By this time he
was exhausted, having been carried down the stream heels
over head. . . . I got him on his feet and led him back in
safety to his gun."

Lamb thought it remarkable that the Americans on the
bank had not fired at him as he struggled to save the gunner,
but now firing became general from the shore; "steady and
galling," it seemed to Colonel Tarleton.

There was confusion near the center of the crossing; a
Tory guide lost his way or was misunderstood, and O'Hara

and his troops plunged straight toward the American campfires, disregarding the 45-degree angle taken by the safer
ford. The water became deeper as they advanced, and progress slowed.

Cornwallis, near the front of the column, rode his horse
onto the bank. As American militiamen ran from the spot,
the General's horse fell dead. A moment or two later Lieutenant Colonel Hall came ashore, fatally wounded.

Robert Henry, of the picket, recognized a man on horseback in the river as a turncoat neighbor, a Tory guide for the
British. The man seemed to be on the point of shooting him
and Henry turned to run, but something stopped him: "I saw
my lame schoolmaster, Beatty, loading his gun by a tree. I
thought I could stand it as long as he could and commenced
loading."

Beatty and Henry each fired at the British file, whose
heads rose just above the bank. The enemy did not return
the fire, and there was quiet for a moment at the ford. Beatty
loaded and Henry was in the process when the teacher fired
and shouted: "It's time to run, Bob!"

Henry peered from behind a tree and saw the British
muskets come down into firing position. There was a volley,
and bark flew from the tree near the boy's head.

Beatty went into the open, and stumbled; a bullet hit him
in the hip. He spraddled on the sandy ground, shouting:
"Run, Bob! Run!"

Henry scurried for the rear and had gone no more than
30 yards when he stumbled into horsemen who were coming
up from the rear, Gen. William Davidson and Col. William
Polk, who had arrived with the larger force from the nearby
ford, unaware that the British had already reached shore.

Henry dodged past them into the woodlands before slowing his pace: "I ran at the top of my speed about one hundred yards, when a thought struck me that the British had no horsemen to follow me."

Joseph Graham, the cavalryman, was with the militia general as the action opened: "At the first alarm those under Genl. Davidson paraded at the horse ford, and Graham's cavalry was ordered to move up briskly, to assist the picket, but by the time they got there, tied their horses, and came up in line to the high bank above the ford, in front of the column, it was within fifty yards of the eastern shore. They took steady and deliberate aim, and fired. The effect was visible. The three first ranks looked thin, and they halted."

Graham saw a horseman among the enemy infantry: "He came pressing up their right flank on the lower side and was distinctly heard giving orders, but we could not hear what they were. The column again got in motion, and kept on."

Thomas Barnett, one of Graham's troopers, loaded and fired at the mounted redcoat officer: "At the flash of the gun both horse and rider went under, and rose down stream. It appeared that the horse had gone over the man. Two or three soldiers caught him and raised him on the upper side. The enemy kept steadily on notwithstanding our fire was well maintained." This casualty was likely Lieutenant Colonel Hall; several other wounded redcoats drifted downstream.

General Davidson, who was now at the water's edge, ordered Graham to take his cavalrymen to a ridge some 200 yards in the rear, as a reserve and as a guard against surprise by British cavalry in the rear. Colonel William Polk's infantry was called to take the post by the river, replacing Graham's men.

Davidson, Polk, and the preacher Thomas McCaule rode

toward the stream as the picket fled by them toward the woods; the riders still had not caught sight of the British below the bank. In the silence which had fallen, two British bugle calls echoed over the water. It was at this moment that the fleeing Robert Henry brushed past Davidson. A British volley crashed through the underbrush and trees. A lone shot was then fired from the British ranks.

Polk turned in his saddle to call to his men: "Fire away, boys! There's help at hand."

Davidson did not ride after Polk but stared briefly at a man on the riverbank who held a smoking rifle in his hands. The General then fell from his horse without uttering a sound, dead of a wound in the breast.* Soldiers who were near him as he fell, including Pvt. Daniel Bryson, could give no assistance; the British were close at hand, and the militiamen were now having trouble firing muskets and rifles in the wet. The militia which Davidson had been trying to put into position rushed away in disorder, "with straight shirttails," one witness said.

The minister, James Hall, who made a futile effort to halt the retreat of his troops, was almost trampled by his frightened congregation. The last American on the site of

---

* Davidson's killer was probably the Tory guide, Frederick Hager, according to the biographer Chalmers G. Davidson (*Piedmont Partisan: The Life and Times of Brigadier-General William Lee Davidson*, Davidson, N.C., Davidson College, 1951). The British historian Charles Stedman, who was near the rear of the attacking column, said (in *The History of the Origin, Progress and Termination of the American War*, 2 vols., London, 1794) that the guide deserted in midstream and fled, in which case he could not have killed Davidson. Neither Cornwallis, Tarleton, nor Roger Lamb mentioned this desertion, and American witnesses were unanimous in asserting that a guide, and not a soldier, fired the fatal shot. Robert Henry, many years later, identified the Tory as one Dick Beal, but others insisted upon Frederick Hager. By family and local traditions, one of Davidson's sons trailed Hager to Arkansas, and killed him there in 1814.

Cowan's Ford was Capt. John Dickey, who fired a final shot at the enemy, turned to inspect the position of his company, and found himself alone.

Colonel Polk carried off his infantry and Graham's cavalry went rearward, but in what their commander recalled as good order. Within two or three hours, all but 300 of the 800 militiamen collected by Davidson had disappeared. The roads were filled with refugees driven from their homes by the sound of cannon fire. Farm families whipped their horses and oxen before loaded carriages and wagons which bore their household goods; the militia swarmed around them, and the old men, women, and children toiled in the mud ruts ahead of the oncoming enemy.

Cornwallis sat a fresh horse at the riverside as the last of his column slogged ashore. When all units were at hand, the column formed and moved a few yards from the stream. There was no opposition in sight; men were ordered to dry their ammunition and guns as best they could about camp-fires. The British count of casualties was not serious: Lieutenant Colonel Hall and three soldiers dead, and thirty-six wounded, all from the light infantry or the grenadiers of the Guards Brigade. The British found two or three wounded American militiamen and took them as prisoners. They did not find the body of General Davidson, which lay in the undergrowth at some distance from the river.

Cornwallis ordered Tarleton to pursue the enemy. He was to turn upstream with his cavalry and the Royal Welsh Fusileers and strike the American rear at Beattie's Ford, enabling Webster to cross. If the militiamen had fled, he was to go after them with all speed. Tarleton was also to scour the back country for reliable information on the location of Greene's other forces.

As Tarleton left the riverside, moving on a track parallel to the stream, a British burial party was already at work in the wet sands, the men laboring in the steady downpour of rain.

His leading squad of dragoons soon brought Tarleton word that the Beattie's Ford position had been abandoned and that there was no opposition to Webster's crossing with the heavy column of baggage wagons. The American militia were streaming away from the river. Tarleton urged his men to greater speed, but the rain-lashed roadway was too much for the Fusileers, who were slowing the column with their struggles. Tarleton left the infantry at a spot five miles from the river and turned east with the cavalry alone. Within three miles he had news from other bedraggled prisoners: The fugitives from the fords were to meet with fresh militia from nearby counties at 2 P.M. at a place known as Torrence's Tavern, which was nearby. Tarleton hurried in that direction.

The tavern was ten miles from the river, at the junction of roads from the nearest Catawba fords; it lay on the main route to Salisbury, a crude inn kept by the widow of Adam Torrence, a victim of the war. The place was a bedlam. The road was jammed with the vehicles of refugees piled high with mattresses, chicken coops, churns, plows, and furnishings, cattle trailing them. From 200 to 300 militia from the fords had gathered here, with many civilians among them. There was busy traffic from the tavern as men bore out pails of the widow's whiskey. A few families were attempting to cook over roadside fires.

Shortly after noon, in the unceasing rain, Tarleton's dragoons appeared. They halted briefly as their commander

studied the landscape and then charged with Tarleton bellowing after them: "Remember the Cowpens!" The young horseman concluded that he faced about five hundred militiamen,
and that their alertness made them formidable foes.

There was one American volley, and then flight; cavalrymen broke the thin American line and swept down the rows
of wagons, hacking at the people and their goods. Mattresses
were ripped and feathers blew in small storms; chickens and
cattle were killed, and there were casualties. Tarleton estimated that there were fifty American dead and many
wounded; he admitted that his own losses were seven dead and
wounded and twenty horses lost.

The American count of losses was ten of their own number dead, some of them unarmed old men, civilians who were
sabered near the tavern; they noted that twelve of the British
were killed or wounded and that fifteen others were dismounted.

Within a few minutes the militia had scattered and the
refugees were hurrying away. Tarleton sent squads of dragoons down each of the roads with orders to break up militia
concentrations, and when these parties had returned, he retreated with his force to the main army, which had gone into
camp five miles from Beattie's Ford.

Cornwallis was pleased with the work of the day—
though he did not yet realize that by the time he forced the
Catawba, Daniel Morgan was already thirty miles ahead of
him and that he had lost rather than gained ground in his hard
marching. He noted in his reports that this was "one of the
most rebellious tracts in America." He praised the troops in
orders:

> The Brigade of Guards will accept his warmest ac-
> knowledgments for the cool and determined bravery

which they showed at the passage of the Catawba when rushing through that long and difficult ford under a galling fire without returning a shot . . . a most pleasing prospect of what may be expected from that distinguished corps.

Of Tarleton's cavalry, the commander said that their action at the tavern "does them infinite honor, and it is a proof that they are determined to preserve the reputation which they have so deservedly acquired in the course of this war."

Nathanael Greene had begun the day at Oliphant's Mill, the site of one of his little supply posts, seventeen miles up-river from Cowan's Ford. In late morning, when he learned that the enemy had crossed the river, he went on horseback to the home of David Carr, a countryman who lived only seven miles beyond Torrence's Tavern on the road to Salisbury. The commander had ordered the militia to meet at this house in case of defeat, but when he arrived, alone, there was no one to meet him. The last of his aides was on the road in the neighborhood, seeking information. Greene remained at Carr's during the afternoon and evening, undetected by British patrols, until about midnight a messenger made it clear that the militia had been scattered and could not be expected to rally—and that all of Cornwallis's force was across the Catawba in position to move toward Salisbury and the Yadkin, which was the next barrier in the chase. Greene now understood that a union of the militia and the main army coming up from South Carolina must be delayed. He rode alone through the night to Salisbury, and as he entered a tavern in that village, he met his hospital director, Dr. William Read. The physician was astonished: "What! Alone, General?"

"Yes, tired, hungry, alone and penniless."

From this encounter grew a local tradition that the mistress of the tavern, Mrs. Elizabeth Steele, gave Greene her life savings, two small bags of coin, for the use of the army.

Morgan's men had already passed this town and were on their way across the flooded Yadkin, which was seven miles beyond. Greene inspected his stores in the village and found 1,700 muskets, all in bad condition. These weapons represented months of effort in collecting them from half-willing officials, but they had been so poorly stored that they were rusted and useless, a treasure lost. Greene was outraged by this and by failure of the militia to appear as he had arranged. He wrote to Baron von Steuben: "These are some of the unhappy effects of defending the Country with Militia from which good Lord deliver us. . . . Oh, that we had in the field as Henry the Fifth said, some few of the merry thousands that are idle at home."

Behind, on the banks of the Catawba, the friends of Gen. William Davidson conducted a macabre funeral service. The nude body had been found on the battlefield, stripped by looters, and was slung over a saddle to be carried to the home of a neighbor, where it was prepared for burial in borrowed clothing. It was taken several miles to Hopewell Presbyterian Church, where Parson McCaule said a brief farewell, and the burial was made by torchlight in the dripping churchyard. Among the tiny group of mourners was the widow, Mary Brevard Davidson, who had left a month-old infant to ride fifteen miles through enemy-held territory in the night.

Except for their commander the militiamen could count only two or three men dead, one of them the schoolmaster, Robert Beatty, who died from the gunshot wound in his hip. There were reports from the river farms to belie British claims of insignificant casualties. Robert Henry, the boy militiaman, saw that the wounded British did not come ashore but were swept downstream in the rapid current. A few days later, he said, neighbors agreed that there were serious British losses: "A great number of the British dead were found on Thompson's fish dam, and in his trap, and numbers lodged on brush, and drifted to the banks. The river stunk with dead carcasses; the British could not have lost less than one hundred men."

The militia cavalryman, Joseph Graham, reported sixteen British wounded under care of a surgeon at a farmhouse near the ford at Cowan's; two British officers followed the main army on litters and there were others riding in the wagon, and among the walking wounded. Two months later Graham found substantiation in a South Carolina newspaper, the *Charleston Gazette:* 31 British dead, 35 wounded. The losses at the ford were never to be determined. There was one the British did not mention: A fine beaver hat, found in the river, was marked "Property of Josiah Martin, Governor." This was a relic of the last of the royal governors, now riding with the invading army in the hope of regaining his domain.

Greene realized that Davidson was a serious casualty; the Carolinian was the only leader who could summon militia of the area from their homes in time of danger. It was Davidson's influence which aroused the men who had won victory at Kings Mountain the preceding autumn, and now that he was dead the men who lived between the Catawba and the Yadkin would not rise until the British army had disappeared. Greene knew that militia support must now come from another region. When he had seen that the few stores at Salisbury were hidden, he rode northward to join Morgan at the Yadkin crossing.

Cornwallis took up the chase at dawn on Feb. 2, impatient at loss of time at Beattie's Ford, where Webster had difficulty crossing his wagons. His Lordship appeared to be losing control of his men, for the march of the army was trailed by columns of smoke during the day. Troops burned the tavern of the widow Torrence, the home of the Brevard family, and several other houses on the route. There were numerous complaints of looting. In the orders of the day, at least, the British commander was indignant:

> Lord Cornwallis is highly displeased that several houses were set on fire during the march this day, a disgrace to the army, and that he will punish with the utmost severity any person. . . found guilty of committing so disgraceful an outrage. His Lordship requests the commanding officers of corps will endeavor to find out the persons who set fire to the houses this day.

This was not enough. As the British moved toward Salisbury and the Yadkin, there were daily scoldings in the orders of Cornwallis:

> Lord Cornwallis has lately received the most shocking complaints of the excesses committed by the troops. He calls on the officers to put a stop to this licentiousness, which must inevitably bring disgrace and ruin on His Majesty's service . . . the blood of the brave and deserving soldiers will be shed in vain, and it will not be even in the power of victory to give success.
> Great complaints having been made of negroes straggling from the line of march, plundering and using violence to the inhabitants, it is Lord Cornwallis' positive orders that no negro shall be suffered to carry arms on any pretense. . . . The Provost Marshal has orders to seize and punish on the spot any negro following the army who may offend against this regulation.

On Feb. 3, after a hard morning's march through overflowing creeks and on miserable roads, Cornwallis reached Salisbury. It was still raining, and the weather was bitterly cold at night. Tories told the British that General Morgan was still crossing the Yadkin seven miles to the north, at Trading Ford, and General O'Hara was hurried off with a special command: the Guards, the Bose Regiment, and the cavalry. His orders were to prevent Morgan's crossing and to destroy captured baggage of the enemy.

The poor roads, rainfall, and darkness kept O'Hara on the march until midnight, when he reached the ford. Rifle fire broke out in the darkness, and the Guards were put into files and sent forward. The enemy disappeared, except for a few who were taken prisoner; these men gave O'Hara bad news: Morgan had already crossed the river, and Greene with him; the Americans had gone across on flatboats which had been gathered from up and down the river and were now on the far side, under a bluff which concealed the retreating army. The few wagons caught by the British belonged to refugees, and the scattered rifle fire had come from a rear guard left to protect them. The last of the Americans had now gone to the north bank.

O'Hara studied the roiling Yadkin with the first light of dawn on Feb. 4 and saw that the brown waters were far more dangerous than those of the Catawba had been. An occasional large tree swept past on the foaming current; it was folly to attempt a fording here. Search parties soon attested to the truth of the tales of prisoners. There was not a boat to be had within many miles. Greene had made effective use of one more river and was now free to join the bands of Morgan and the main army approaching from South Carolina. Cornwallis must seek another route.

By now the British guns were up, and, as if in petulant rage, O'Hara turned them on the position of the Americans hiding across the river. The balls fell on the bluff without harm, but a few of them fell on or quite near a cabin whose roof was barely visible to the redcoat gunners.

Dr. William Read was with Greene in this cabin and noted with amazement that the Quaker General seemed oblivious to the cannon fire and to the ricocheting iron balls falling among large rocks nearby. Greene was writing dispatches. Read wrote:

> In a few minutes the clapboards were flying from the roof in all directions. But still the General wrote on, nor seemed to notice anything but his dispatches, and the innumerable applications which were made to him from various quarters. His pen never rested but when a new visitor arrived, and then the answer was given with calmness and precision, and the pen immediately resumed.

Greene wrote to everyone of influence who might be of help to the retreating army. He asked Colonel Pickens to hang in the British rear with his guerrillas; he wrote von Steuben urging that men be hurried down from Virginia; he wrote Jefferson with the same plea. He ordered his commissary officers to move stores from the Moravian towns, in the path of a possible British thrust upriver. He called his quartermaster, Lt. Col. Edward Carrington, who had returned from Virginia. He ordered Dr. Read to organize a company of wounded and sick to guard hospital stores and prisoners on the march northward.

Dr. Read also visited Morgan in his tent during the night on the bank of the Yadkin. He found him lying in a pile of leaves, covered with a blanket, and "rheumatic from head to feet." Read attempted treatment and was chagrined an hour or so later when he came upon Morgan at the riverside, directing the movement of a scouting party.

While Greene was organizing a rear guard and sending new instructions for General Huger to march to Guilford Courthouse with the main army, Morgan put his force on the road north. During the night it had been uncertain that the army could move the artillery because of the soft roads, which were bottomless; an overnight freeze hardened the ruts, and the big guns moved off after the column.

Greene got reports from spies that Cornwallis, now in Salisbury, was preparing to move, and in his dispatch to Huger the Quaker said: "If Ld. Cornwallis knows his true interest he will pursue our army. If he can disperse that, he completes the reduction of the State, and without that, he can do nothing to effect."

The army marched a short distance from the Yadkin to the forks of Abbott's Creek, whence it watched the British in temporary safety. Greene now needed every advantage of the river and ground, for the Virginia militia of Gen. Edward Stevens, their time up, insisted upon going home in the hour of emergency. Stevens reviled them as cowards:

> After crossing the Yadkin we could not have paraded a greater force than eight hundred for action, if even that including Militia and all, and a great part of the number was the Militia under me whose times were out. I saw the greatest necessity of these men remaining a few days till the troops from General Greene's camp could get up, and this the General requested of me to endeavor to bring about.
>
> I had them paraded and addressed the subject. But to my great mortification and astonishment scarce a man would agree to it, and gave for an answer he was a good soldier that served his time out. If the Salvation of the Country had depended on their staying ten or fifteen days,

I don't believe they would have done it. Militia won't do. Their greatest study is to rub through their tour of duty with whole bones.

After a night at Abbott's, Greene learned that the British had moved westward, up the Yadkin toward the shallow fords, and he moved once more, abandoning an earlier plan to march to Salem, one of the Moravian towns. Morgan was by now far to the north of him, settling in the village of Guilford Courthouse, a cluster of log houses with a population of about two hundred, all centered around the tiny courthouse, the jail, and a coppersmith's shop. Greene had marked it on his map as a likely place to make a stand, a way point on the great north-south road through the State.

The Quaker had another disturbing letter from Morgan on Feb. 6, written from Guilford Courthouse:

I arrived here last evening and sent a number of prisoners that were here to join the main body. About 4000 pound of salted pork and bacon is promised me, corn meal equivalent, forage, etc.

I am much indisposed with pains and to add to my misfortunes am violently attacked with the Piles, so that I can scarcely sit upon my horse. This is the first time that I ever experienced that disorder, and from the idea I had of it, sincerely prayed that I might never know what it was. When I set everything in as good a train as I can respecting provisions, I shall try to move on more slowly to some safe retreat, and try to recover. . . .

Greene left a small rear guard at Abbott's Creek and rode toward Morgan at Guilford, realizing that at last he was on the point of losing his lieutenant.

There was one note of cheer in the gloom of Feb. 8, for dispatches from the backcountry reported that militia were assembling once more, ready to do their duty. Greene replied that they should be held in readiness until Cornwallis made his move. He wrote some optimistic letters to guerrilla leaders, promising to strike the British, but for the moment he waited. If Cornwallis circled far up the Yadkin for a crossing, Huger would march on to Guilford as planned; ammunition and flints and other supplies were hurried in to the court-house village. Scouts hung on the fringes of the British army, ordered to report any sign of movement.

Cornwallis slaughtered a small herd of cattle on Feb. 4 near the Yadkin ford outside Salisbury, and the men ate as they waited for a decision from their commander. Orders warned the Brigade of Guards that in any future movement they were expected to form ranks and move within a quarter of an hour. Officers were forbidden to pitch tents here, though they got "a small dividend of beer." On Feb. 6, convinced that the Yadkin would not fall far enough to permit his passage at this spot, Cornwallis turned upstream toward the shallow fords, attempting to conceal his departure until the last moment. His orders were stern: The pickets were not to be called in until fifteen minutes before the march began, and the army was to move off "without noise," the infantry in double files, ready for instant action.

There was an unscheduled delay. A party of American guerrillas under Col. Francis Locke lay in wait at Grant's Creek, not far from Salisbury. They so stubbornly defended a bridge that the British reconnaissance party under Tarleton, composed of cavalry and the Fusileers, was held up for three hours and forced to make a flanking march upstream. Locke, who had been reported dead by British scouts, partially destroyed the bridge and forced its repair by the British. The only casualty was a wounded American.

Tarleton soon pushed riders ahead to the Yadkin's upper fords and sent word to Cornwallis that the way was clear. His Lordship issued one day's rum ration to the troops but issued orders that any officer who permitted looting, or wanton destruction on the march up the river would be regarded "in a more criminal light than the persons who commit these scandalous crimes."

The orders of Feb. 9, in camp at Salem, read:

Lord Cornwallis having perceived that many soldiers are coming into town, and seemingly for the purpose of getting liquor; he begs it may be told to the men that if they commit such irregularities, he shall not think it necessary to trouble the commissaries in providing any more rum for them.

The following day Cornwallis planned to make another leap at the disappearing army of Greene, perhaps to take it by surprise. He moved the marching hour forward from 6 A.M. to 5:30—and on the night of Feb. 14, finding that he was still falling behind, ordered the army to cover twenty-five miles the next day, leaving behind all baggage except canteens.

He moved swiftly toward the Dan River, hoping once more to pin the Americans against the bank of an impassable stream. He was now very far from his base, but he was certain that he could cut off Greene from the upper fords of the Dan, and that the Quaker could not again call upon the miracle of the boats. His Lordship thought the climax of the campaign was at hand. He still sought more speed from his column, but its recent performance was a great improvement over the marches of January. From the first to the fifteenth of February, the British marched 230 miles, as compared with about a third of that distance in the previous fortnight.

One More River

O N THE RAW MORNING OF FEB. 6 GENERALS ISAAC HUGER and Harry Lee led the main army into Guilford Courthouse, a long, halting train of misery, the men in rags and in many cases barefoot, the wagons with leaning wheels, drawn by bony animals in patched and broken harness.

Nathanael Greene watched calmly as the troops came in to their cold camp, but he wrote George Washington immediately:

... The miserable situation of the troops for want of clothing has rendered the march the most painful imaginable, with hundreds tracking the ground with bloody feet. Your feelings for the suffering soldiers, had you been here, must have been shocked on the occasion. . . .

Myself and my aides are almost worn out with fatigue, which prevents my giving Your Excellency more frequent and particular accounts of our movements. The army is in good spirits notwithstanding its suffering and excessive fatigue.

On this day many veterans of the northern fighting thought of Valley Forge. The army's meager medical supplies were used to treat Huger's men, hundreds of whom had torn and frostbitten feet. These men had slept four to a blanket on the cold and wet ground of their camps on the march from South Carolina and were plagued by a variety of complaints; wagons were filled with the sick.

Morgan's own march had been painful enough (one of his men wrote that the last day passed with "every step being up to our knees in mud—it raining on us all the way"), but the condition of Huger's troops was obviously serious. Yet there was little time for rest. Greene now had about twenty-three hundred men. Of these, 500 were militia, including survivors from Cowan's Ford; 270 were cavalry, which Harry Lee thought "of the best quality."

Huger's report was not encouraging. After many long marches without desertions, men were now streaming away so rapidly that they could not be stopped. One company of 300 had dwindled to 36 within a week, and, equally serious, the deserters had carried off muskets of Continental issue.

Supply officers found shoes in the village for some of the men who had come from Cheraw barefoot, but, as Sgt. Maj. William Seymour of the Delaware regiment said dolefully, "not half enough." The fighting to come must be borne by a band of ragamuffins.

Greene held a council of war in the remote village, probably in the courthouse itself, a crude frame structure in a woods clearing of what had so lately been Indian country. The commander was anxious to turn and give battle to Cornwallis, and this place appealed to him as a defensive position. Despite the condition of his army, the Quaker argued persuasively that they must fight. If they retreated into Virginia, the Whigs of the Carolinas would be plunged into despair and the Tory raiders would rise once more. This would mean

the virtual loss of these two States. It was soon clear that his
lieutenants did not agree.

His officers were aggressive men, but they persuaded the
commander that he must march on northward, to the next
region of safety, beyond the Dan River on the Virginia border.

Spies said that Cornwallis was twenty-five miles to the
west, at Salem. The British were thus nearer to the shallow
upper reaches of the Dan than the Americans. The highest
deep crossing of that river, known as Dix's Ferry, was equidistant from the two camps. The British were estimated to
have 2,500 men, but they were all dependable veterans, still
well-equipped, against whom the worn men of Greene would
accomplish little.

Even the pain-racked Morgan agreed that the army was
in no condition for attack, and the others were unanimous:
Huger and Harry Lee, William Washington, John Eager
Howard, Otho Williams, and Edward Carrington. When
Greene reluctantly agreed that they must flee once more, rac-
ing for the last river barrier in the Carolinas, the officers turned
to their maps.

It was clear that this race would be the closest of the
campaign, since they no longer had the advantage of distance
over the British, and the country was open as far as the Dan.
Colonel Carrington provided the key: About seventy miles
to the northeast, farther downstream on the Dan, were two
good crossings, Irwin's and Boyd's Ferries. These were only
four miles apart, and the army could use both for its escape.
Carrington could hurry to the upper crossing at Dix's Ferry,
take its boats downstream, and help put the troops across before the British could arrive. Greene's foresight had also provided other boats, some of them hauled in wagons at great

sacrifice. If the army could outrun the enemy in the next few days, Carrington would provide a safe crossing.

Greene responded immediately: The main army would march directly for the lower ferries of the Dan; the vanguard would leave the next day. A light corps of 700 picked men would be detached to move slowly in front of the British army, annoying with skirmishing, raids, and captures, taking every opportunity to delay the enemy. This was more than a rear guard. It would move northward on a road roughly parallel to Greene's route, staying between the army and Cornwallis. The force was made up of 240 of William Washington's horsemen, 280 Continental infantrymen under John Eager Howard, and 60 mountain riflemen, sharpshooters all, under Col. William Campbell.

This small force was ordered to shield the army at all costs, to move swiftly, destroy bridges, and remove horses and provisions from the path of the enemy. Greene offered command of the band to Morgan. The Old Wagoner shook his head: He could no longer ride a horse, much less embark on another campaign. He must go home to Virginia to seek relief from his sciatica and his homely new ailment. Others must finish the fight.

Harry Lee detected impatience in their commander, though Morgan's physical condition was well known: "Greene listened with reluctance to the excuse, and endeavored to prevail on him to recede from his determination." He did not move Morgan. A few minutes later, when Morgan left the council, Greene sent his intimate friend Harry Lee after him, with instructions to make one last effort to persuade the Old Wagoner to remain.

Lee tried for a long time to hold Morgan, and when other arguments failed, he said:

"If you retire now, when we must do or die, people will say that you're not the patriot you once were. Have you thought of your reputation? Men always think that a successful officer who leaves his army in a crisis has begun to think of the prospect of defeat. Do you know what they'll say of you—that you won your fame by accident!"

Lee thought for a moment that he had persuaded the veteran: "These observations appeared to touch the feelings of Morgan; for a moment he paused; then discovered a faint inspiration to go through the impending conflict; but finally returned to his original decision."

Lee gave up the attempt and returned to Greene with word that they had lost the victor of Cowpens. Morgan requested retirement from the army and was issued a brief document:

> General Morgan, of the Virginia Line, has leave of absence until he recovers his health, so as to be able to take the field again.
>
> Nath Greene

The Quaker then turned to the problems of the march. He gave command of the screening force to Col. Otho Williams of Maryland. The main body left Guilford Courthouse on the morning of Feb. 10. Williams held his party in the village for a short time, then moved westward toward the Moravian village of Salem, where the enemy had camped.

On the day Greene left Guilford, Morgan moved on his journey up the Shenandoah Valley to Winchester, Virginia. He traveled with two companions, Nat and Toby, Negro slaves captured at Cowpens who would serve him until his death. He moved slowly, halting to spend nights at isolated farmhouses and jolting part of the way in a carriage. The army was seldom out of his thoughts.

It was less than five months since Morgan had come to North Carolina as a volunteer, just after the disastrous battle of Camden. He had with difficulty (and without the support of George Washington) been raised to the rank of brigadier general. He had been in independent command for most of those dark months and, by winning the most brilliant victory on the southern front, made possible Greene's campaign of maneuver. He had saved his prisoners and spoils and marched his small band to a safe junction with the main army. He could now foresee victory in the south. When he stopped for a few days to rest at the home of a friend, Brig. Gen. Robert Lawson of the Virginia militia, he wrote to Greene: "As the militia are collecting fast, I have advised General Lawson to go too, and give you all in his power. . . . I wish I was able to give you my aid; but find I get worse." Lawson was soon to report to Greene with a large band of men, adding much strength to the army.

A few days later, when he stopped at the home of another friend, Carter Harrison, Morgan wrote Greene more fully:

> I have been doctoring these several days, thinking to be able to take the field again. But I find I get worse. My pains now are accompanied by a fever every day. I expect Lord Cornwallis will push you until you are obliged to fight him, on which much will depend. You have, from what I can see, a great number of militia. If they fight, you will beat Cornwallis; if not, he will beat you, and perhaps cut your regulars to pieces, which will be losing all our hopes.
>
> I am informed that among the militia will be found a number of old soldiers. I think it would be advisable to select them from among the militia and put them in the ranks with the regulars; select the riflemen also, and fight

them on the flanks, under enterprising officers who are acquainted with that kind of fighting; and put the militia in the center, with some picked troops in their rear, with orders to shoot down the first man that runs. If anything will succeed, a disposition of this kind will. I hope you will not look on this as dictating, but it is my opinion on a matter I am much concerned in.

Less than a month later, this plan was used by Greene in the major battle of the campaign; it was essentially the pattern of the battle at Cowpens.

Greene missed Morgan. Though Harry Lee had reservations about the patriotic ardor of the forty-five-year-old sufferer, the Quaker had none: "Great generals are scarce," he said. "There are few Morgans to be found." The self-taught soldier of the frontier had left to the self-taught military scholar of Rhode Island the unpromising task of halting the invader.

Lord Cornwallis had found the village of Salem to his liking, a neat hillside town of mellow brick houses and a passable tavern. The Moravians were civil enough, "mild and hospitable," Colonel Tarleton said. The British paused overnight, took out a good supply of meal and bread, and hurried into the trail of the American army. Tory camp followers and hangers-on looted Salem and nearby villages when the regulars had gone—but there was worse to come. On the fourth day a band of Whig guerrillas arrived to a warm Moravian welcome; the raiders robbed their hosts of almost everything left to them, halting people on the streets to strip them of clothing, horses, and other valuables. The Germans sent off a bitter dispatch to Greene, complaining of the treatment they got in return for providing him with a base of supplies.

Scouts and spies assured Cornwallis that Greene could escape only by the upper reaches of the Dan, where his troops could wade; the winter weather had so swollen the Dan that it was beyond fording downstream—and there was not the slightest chance that the Americans could find enough boats to set across even a small part of their army. His Lordship had been forced to waste several days in marching up the Yadkin to pursue Greene, and his feat of mounting two men to each horse for greater speed in the early chase had come to naught. He was determined that he would cut the Americans off before they got into Virginia. He moved north, his vanguard composed of the deadly German Yagers and the cavalry of Tarleton's Legion. He had not long to grope for the enemy.

On his first day out of Salem, Feb. 10, Cornwallis ran into trouble: The vanguard reported that the way was blocked. There was desultory rifle fire, and the British took to cover to await orders. Cornwallis halted progress until the long column could pull itself together; he looked anxiously over the terrain in his front but could make out little or nothing of his opposition. There was rebel infantry and cavalry, but whether Greene's main body was at hand, he could not determine. For fear of ambush he waited until the regiments were massed in column, then pressed on; the roadblock moved ahead of him with a stubborn slowness. Cornwallis lost several hours during the day, without inflicting a loss on the enemy. His vanguard remained in sight of the American rear until nightfall.

Colonel Otho Holland Williams had been picked by Daniel Morgan to take his place as commander of the screening force. The Marylander was a veteran of some of the hardest

fighting of the war; he had gone to Boston with the Frederick
County rifle corps in 1775, had marched with the fateful
Canadian expedition, and had been captured the following
autumn when Hessians overwhelmed riflemen at Fort Washington on the Hudson. Once out of prison, he had come south
as colonel of the Sixth Maryland Continentals and was one of
the last men to leave the scene of defeat at Camden, when
South Carolina had been swept by the British.

Like Morgan, he was a sharp-eyed field soldier who saw
to the needs of his men. His men found him strict in discipline
but warm and human in the manner of Greene; some thought
him vain, but a good officer who did not leave men in doubt
as to where they stood. He fought the British in the last phase
of the race to the Dan like a master.

The skirmish of Feb. 10 was only the opening display of
the talents of Williams. When he had snarled the enemy
column and forced its delay, he pulled back deftly toward a
middle road between Greene's main army, which was to his
east, and Cornwallis, who was to his west, and rear. Williams
clung to this blocking position as he retreated, entering the
middle road near the end of the day, when he had baffled
Cornwallis.

The corps was driven hard all day, and night only increased hardships. Williams kept himself at a distance from
the British out of fear of a night attack; the enemy column
moved until late. It would be fatal to allow Cornwallis to
encircle him while his troops slept in camp, thus exposing the
main army to attack. So Williams sent out strong patrols, infantry and cavalry, and kept them at it all night. Heavy pickets
surrounded the camp.

Half of the American troops were assigned to night duty
every other night, so that the men got but six hours of rest in

forty-eight. Harry Lee thought the troops "in fine spirits and good health" in spite of this regimen, and morale was high.

At 3 A.M. on Feb. 11 Williams had the force moving once more, hurrying forward in an effort to give the men time for a leisurely breakfast before the enemy caught up. It was the only meal of the day, during the whole of the retreat to the river. At each stop, every man not assigned to duty fell exhausted to the ground and slept, without thought of food.

On the third day the British changed course. Williams concluded that enemy intelligence had picked up news of their true destination, for Cornwallis made a sharp right turn during the day, entering a long causeway through a swampy area which led to the road to Dix's Ferry, the one used by Williams. Tarleton's Legion was in front at this hour—far in front. Lee's Legion was in the American rear.

The morning was cold and drizzly, and Harry Lee was forward, eating a breakfast of corncakes in a farmhouse with the staff, when a farmer rode up in great haste on a worn pony. He reported the British were in their road, and half an hour ago had been only four miles behind. Colonel Williams gave a casual order, and a section of cavalry was sent back to investigate. When another report of enemy progress came in, Lee was sent with reinforcements. The farmer followed, mounted on a dragoon horse; Lee's bugler, one Gillies, a twelve-year-old boy too small to carry a sword, trailed them on the farmer's old horse.

There was a clash of cavalry in the roadway, and the leading American section fled. Lee's reinforcements galloped up, too late to save Gillies from the British swords—but eighteen of twenty British riders were killed, wounded, or captured, and those who escaped were chased on orders from Lee: "Give them no quarter! Kill the last of them."

Lee was on the point of hanging the British dragoon captain in command when the enemy's main body approached and he was forced to send his prisoners forward to Williams. Eighteen British dragoons lay in the road for Cornwallis to bury as he passed. The bugler Gillies was Lee's only casualty; his body was left in woods by the road for neighbors to bury.

Later in the morning there was a dispatch from Colonel Williams: The main army should be nearing the Dan, and the screening force would abandon its road during the day, shifting eastward in the tracks of Greene, marching for Irwin's Ferry. The infantry was hurrying to get far in advance of the enemy, so that the men could get a good night's sleep. Lee improved on the order. He left a small cavalry guard in the rear of Williams and rode cross-country on a short route to the new road, in hopes of completing the interrupted breakfast at some farmhouse.

Lee led his troopers down a little-used country lane, leaving only a few pickets, and went into a farmhouse. Firing broke out while the horses were unbridled, and Lee was about to eat his bacon and cornbread. There was a race for the roadway—for Cornwallis, having detected Williams's move, had cut across country by the route Lee had taken. The cavalrymen held off the oncoming enemy for a few minutes, long enough for Lee's troop to escape over a bridge into the main road. For more than a mile, as the chase slowed, the Americans rode within full sight of the pursuing British, as if both were part of the same moving army.

It was on the next morning, Feb. 14, that Cornwallis ordered his army to prepare for a twenty-five-mile march during the day, stripping the men of everything but arms and canteens in an effort to overtake Greene.

General O'Hara pressed the vanguard close to Williams's

screen, but though there were many moments during the day when it seemed that there must be a pitched battle to hold off the redcoats, the hours passed with the same skilled skirmishing which had marked Williams's course from the start. Lee was forced to restrain his young officers, who wanted to make flanking movements against the exposed British van. When creeks were forded, Cornwallis rushed his men forward with even greater speed to cut off the enemy, but was always too late. As Lee said, "Their useless efforts were gradually discontinued," and near the end of the day the armies had settled to a rapid, steady march.

The Americans had no relief at night, for Cornwallis kept up the chase for hours after dark. Harry Lee did not forget this evening:

"The night was dark, the roads deep, the weather cold, and the air humid."

Williams put the cavalry in his front and left the rear to the infantry of Lee's Legion. About eight o'clock the army sighted hundreds of fires in the woods ahead and was dismayed. No one doubted that this was Greene's army in camp, helpless before an attack of the oncoming enemy. Talk passed swiftly down the column and reached Williams: The men wanted to turn and make a stand before the whole British army, giving Greene's men a few minutes to escape. The Colonel was moved, but he hestitated and, when he thought of Greene's letter, concluded that this must be an old campsite, and that the Quaker was now on the banks of the Dan. Within a few minutes the vanguard found that the campfires were abandoned and danger was past. The rearguard soon reported that the British had halted for the night, and Williams went into camp. The screening force and the army of Cornwallis were now within forty miles of the river.

The Quaker had troubles of his own. On the second day of his march he wrote a North Carolina general that only 120 of the State's militia were left with the army "to render the regulars the least assistance." When he awoke on the following day, Greene found that forty of the remainder had deserted during the night, led by their officers.

Greene wrote anxiously to Williams: "You have the flower of the army. Do not expose the men too much lest our situation grow more critical."

By 4 A.M. on the next day Greene had sent Williams the dispatch ordering a change of route:

"Follow our route, as a division of our forces might encourage the enemy to push us further than they will dare to if we are together. I have not slept four hours since you left me, so great has been my solicitation to prepare for the worst. I have great reason to believe that one of Tarleton's officers was in our camp night before last."

The Quaker had written ex-Governor Patrick Henry, as a last resort, asking his aid in assembling 1,500 Virginia troops to meet him on the Dan:

> . . . My force is too inconsiderable to march the limits of the enemy's depredations, or in any wise to check the rapidity of their march through this unhappy country. My duty compels me to retreat. . . . Your influence in Virginia, properly exercized at this important period, may terminate the war. . . .
>
> The Present moment is so big with the most important consequences and requires the greatest and most spirited exertions. You, I know, are equal to them. . . .

To militia leaders of the region he wrote even more imploringly:

Let me conjure you, my countrymen, to fly to arms, and repair to headquarters without loss of time, and bring with you ten days' provisions. . . . If you will not face the approaching dangers, your country is inevitably lost. . . .

The little sleep the Quaker did snatch during this week was troubled. He rode with South Carolina's wandering governor, John Rutledge, and one night they could find no shelter except a roadside hovel. They awoke during the night and quarreled, each accusing the other of kicking in his sleep. When the commotion continued, candlelight revealed that a hog had crawled into bed with them to escape the chill rain.

Another of the commander's companions was the supply master, Col. William R. Davie, who desperately herded wagons of stores ahead of the army, preparing for the coming weeks. The campaign dazzled Davie—"a continued display of military science in marches, counter marches and positions, Lord Cornwallis exhausting all the stratagems of war."

Colonel Williams and his men had a brief rest in the night of Feb. 13–14. The British moved once more at midnight and were soon driving in the mounted pickets of the rear. The dark, wet night, with the ground freezing underfoot, was passed in pursuit more rapid than before, and the armies continued through the mists of dawn and for hours beyond before the first halt was called. Each army paused an hour for breakfast.

Soon after this halt a horseman came to Williams with a dispatch from Greene: The main army had crossed the Dan. Carrington's boats had saved them—and Thaddeus Kosciusko was already throwing up breastworks on the north bank of the river. The rear guard broke into cheers as the news passed.

The British guessed the cause of the whoops, but they pressed on without respite.

At 3 P.M. Williams took the infantry on a quick march to the river, now fourteen miles away, and Lee was left in the rear with his Legion; Williams crossed the Dan about sunset, and Lee, falling back slowly, reached the ferry at about 9 P.M. His crossing of the swift river was uneventful, except for some frightened horses which fled and had to be chased down in darkness. There was a noisy welcome at Greene's headquarters on the northern bank; the main army now lay with its head across the Banister River to the north and its rear on the Dan.

In the next morning's fog British campfires flickered on the southern bank. Greene did not exult. He wrote Thomas Jefferson that day:

> On the Dan River, almost fatigued to death, having had a retreat to conduct for upwards of two hundred miles, maneuvering constantly in the face of the enemy, to give time for the militia to turn out and get off our stores. . . .

But to von Steuben the Quaker confessed:

> We have been astonishingly successful in our late great and fatiguing retreat, and have never lost in one instance anything of the least value.

George Washington sent his congratulations:

> You may be assured that your retreat before Cornwallis is highly applauded by all ranks, and reflects much honor on your military abilities.

Even the enemy was complimentary. Banastre Tarleton said:

> Owing to an excellent disposition, which was attended with some fortunate contingencies, General Greene passed

the whole army over the river . . . without their receiving any material detriment from the King's troops. Every measure of the Americans, during their march from the Catawba to Virginia, was judiciously designed and vigorously executed.

The British had marched almost forty miles in the last twenty-four hours of the fruitless chase, their most vigorous move in the crossing of North Carolina, in which Cornwallis had spent a month. Greene prepared to meet the enemy if they attempted to cross the Dan, but within a day the Quaker concluded that the pursuers would not come. Officers studied the fresh breastworks of the Americans, foragers went out from the British camp, and the main body lay, briefly watching.

Cornwallis had put an additional 150 miles between his army and the nearest base of supplies. Food and ammunition were not plentiful, and his troops were becoming poorly clad. His plight had become serious. The Earl was convinced that he could not plunge into the populous and defiant Virginia counties. He would seek supplies and men.

His Lordship had been overmatched against Greene, Morgan, the wilderness winter, and the rugged backcountry through which he had come. He had rather recklessly opened a campaign in the heart of winter, in a region strange to him; his movements since the battle of Cowpens had only the aim of overtaking Greene's army. At the start, the Quaker knew no more of the southern frontier than the British professional, but he had made himself familiar with its chief features in ways astonishing even to his most devoted lieutenants. Greene had been able to prepare for emergencies at the vital river crossings, where the chase came to climax. His strategy had been more flexible, and the Quaker had not hesitated to improvise to meet new situations.

Before Cowpens, the British had laid a careful plan of campaign, and its conception was that of Cornwallis. When stung by the loss at Cowpens, he had abandoned his plans and lunged off after his prey; yet he seemed to permit sheer circumstance to dictate his movements, for he moved now slowly and then swiftly, without pattern. His Lordship had been frustrated at every turn, up to the moment he reached the Dan River and found all the Americans safely across and every boat removed from the southern bank for miles in either direction. Charles Cornwallis had begun to learn a bitter lesson of military science: In irregular warfare, the regular force fares ill.

Cornwallis's errors on the route had been costly:

First, he had moved from South Carolina without time for resting the large reinforcement hurried in by General Leslie, its men worn by difficult passage of the swamps.

Second, he had burned his heavy baggage at Ramsour's Mill to gain speed, but to little advantage. He had deprived himself of a certain supply but was still forced to hold down his pace to that of the big guns—which proved to be as ungainly as the largest wagons.

Third, he had failed to send back to his base in South Carolina the large band of women and Negro camp followers who swarmed about his column under the guise of serving his officers. Though he punished and scolded looters, the Earl did not strip them of their loot, further slowing his march.

Fourth, though he had blindly followed the reports of spies and scouts in the last phase, Cornwallis had disregarded the advice of scouts who had lain near Greene's camp, and was then led on a false trail by Otho Williams.

The British rested on the Dan for four days, foraging and reorganizing companies, and the orders of Feb. 16 appointed "a halting day" so that the men could wash clothing and clean themselves. The weather was still bitter.

Cornwallis set up guards at nearby mills, where meal and flour were ground for the troops. On Feb. 17 he once more lectured his men on atrocities:

> Lord Cornwallis is very sorry to be again obliged to call the attention of the Officers of the Army to the repeated orders against plundering . . . he assures the Officers that if their duty to their King and their country and their feelings for humanity are not sufficient to enforce their obedience to them, he must, however reluctant, make use of such power as the military laws have placed in his hands.

In an effort to check looting his Lordship limited each regimental quartermaster to eight Negroes for his forage gangs, and each of them must carry a ticket signed by officers. Any Negro without a ticket was to be arrested; Negroes must also have tickets for any horses in their possession. This limited exertion on record, Cornwallis turned to the southeast, and by easy marches moved to the capital of North Carolina, the village of Hillsboro.

On Feb. 21 Cornwallis raised the Royal Standard in the town and issued a proclamation calling for reinforcements:

> Whereas, it has pleased the Divine Providence to prosper the operations of His Majesty's arms in driving the rebel arm out of this province, and whereas it is His Majesty's most gracious wish to rescue his faithful and loyal subjects from the cruel tyranny under which they have groaned for several years, I have thought it proper to issue this proclamation,
> To invite all such faithful and loyal subjects to repair, without loss of time, with their arms and three days' provisions, to the Royal Standard, now erected at Hillsboro, where they will meet with the most friendly reception.
> And I do hereby assure them that I am ready to concur

with them in effectual measures for suppressing the remains
of rebellion in this province, and for the re-establishment of
good order and constitutional government. . . .

Josiah Martin, the deposed Royal governor who still
traveled with the army, was busy in the town, drumming up
volunteers, and the Tory newspapers soon boasted that more
than 700 men had come in from the country to the colors—
all in one day. They came, but they did not volunteer. When
the farm people had inspected the lord's army and heard news
of the campaign, they returned to their farms. Cornwallis
was disappointed in the loyal men of the State: "Their numbers are not so great as had been represented and their friend-
ship was only passive."

The troops were busy for a few days, repairing harness
and uniforms, holding inspections for weapons, flints, and
ammunition, and conducting forage parties into the country.
Hides were issued and shoes were made. Food was scarce, and
householders were robbed.

To keep the men at work, Cornwallis set hundreds of
them to paving the streets of the village near his artillery park;
the stone paving covered rutted tracks in the center of the
village.

Cornwallis lengthened his stay in Hillsboro with the
discovery of a treasure, a stock of salt pork and beef and a
few live hogs, but this was soon gone. The historian Stedman
led a squad of men from house to house, searching for food
and bearing it off amid the curses and plaints of citizens.
Sergeant Lamb of the Welsh Fusileers noted that it was impossible for the army to live long in this place, since provisions were so scanty. Some of the best of the British draft
horses were slaughtered to feed the men and the great carcasses roasted over fires in the camp.

News from scouts did not improve things for the British:

Greene's army still lay over the Dan, no more than two good marches to the northwest; the enemy army was growing and showing new confidence. American raiding parties were pushing back into the State. There was a sudden chill among the native Tories in Hillsboro.

A further hint of his perilous situation was given in another of his Lordship's fatherly orders:

> It is with great concern that Lord Cornwallis hears every day reports of the soldiers being taken by the enemy, in consequence of their straggling out of camp in search of whiskey. . . .

He warned that anyone taken would spend "some years in a loathsome prison, subject to the bitter insults of the rebels, for the chance of a momentary gratification of his appetite."

The power of the British army extended no more than a musket shot from the camp of the Earl; no redcoat commanded more ground than he stood upon.

The Ground Is Chosen

VIRGINIANS SEEMED TO VALUE THEIR FINE HORSES ABOVE their freedom, and for some days Nathanael Greene skirmished with them over mounts for his cavalry.

Thomas Jefferson had not forgotten the rights of the States, even with the enemy lying on the border of Virginia. Greene had no more than entered the State than militiamen came out by the thousands, but when they collected, county lieutenants disbanded them, saying that the law did not require their services. Several hundred went to Greene's camp at Halifax Courthouse, but they had no guns and were sent home.

Governor Jefferson had at last called up a fourth of the militia of the region, however, and promised to call more. A search was made for guns.

Greene wrote Jefferson on Feb. 16 while the British were still within sight of the Dan crossings, asking for emergency powers to collect horses, supplies, and men. He was still uncertain as to whether Cornwallis would cross the river and press for an engagement in Virginia, and mounted patrols had to watch the enemy. Many of his cavalrymen were walking, since horses had been worn out on the long march. He had to have horses immediately.

Jefferson responded generously: "Take Horses to mount your cavalry, and I will attempt to have it justified."

Greene sent William Washington to work. He was to treat the Virginians "with tenderness" but was to impress all the horses he needed to fill out the troops and make the cavalry effective once more. He would see that proper receipts were given to owners from whom horses were taken and a true evaluation placed upon them. He would explain civilly the need of the army and the plight of the State and nation. The first collection of horses brought screams of protest from the countryside. Greene learned that the best horses of the area had been taken, their value running to from $800 to $1,000 per head, including some prize stallions. Washington was urged to make future raids "with great delicacy," and to take fewer horses. The impressment continued, with little change, until the troopers were properly mounted once more.

Jefferson sent a warm protest to Greene:

> Instead of soothing the minds of the people and softening the harsh act of taking their valuable Horses by Force, it has been frequently accompanied by defiances of civil Power and the Circumstances of personal Irritation . . . free People think they have a right to an Explanation of the Circumstances which give rise to the Necessity under which they suffer.

Other Virginians also regarded Greene's army as something less than an ally. One high-ranking officer who was expected to raise militia begged off, saying that his duties on the governor's Council were too great. Greene's appeal to Jefferson was pointed enough: "The army is all that the States have to depend on for their political existence."

The Quaker had information from the British camp that made the situation darker than Jefferson could realize. After he heard from his scouts who lay near Hillsboro, Greene wrote:

We have the most unequivocal and full evidence of the disaffection of a great part of this State. The enemy have raised seven independent companies in a single day; and we have the mortification to find that most of the prisoners we take are inhabitants of America.

Resistance to Greene was short-lived, for the common people of Virginia were aroused by the approach of the enemy. Brigadier General Edward Stevens, who had conducted the Cowpens prisoners northward with his homeward-bound troops, dismissed his men and stored their arms at Pittsylvania Courthouse. When he learned of the crossing of the Dan, Stevens mustered a few veterans, with arms, and hurried to headquarters. Greene placed him in command of Virginia militia and helped him to form the nucleus of a brigade; many of these men were veterans of long fighting.

Greene also wrote to military and civil officials throughout North Carolina and Virginia, urging them to send men; he tried to pit the States against each other in a race to raise the greatest number, telling Governor Nash of North Carolina that Virginia was responding nobly to his call, and that Carolinians were rare in his ranks. He already had the promise of important aid from the western counties, where the mountain men who had fought at Kings Mountain were now gathering.

The troops were now well-fed for the first time in many weeks, and wagons rolled in daily from the untouched countryside around Halifax. There were a few days of rest.

On Feb. 17, almost incredibly, Greene announced to the army his plans for a limited offensive: On the next day, Harry Lee with his cavalry and Col. Andrew Pickens with two companies of Maryland infantry and the South Carolina militia would recross the Dan and hang on the fringes of the British army. The Quaker ordered them to stay as near to Cornwallis as they dared, cutting his communications with the country and taking or killing all who strayed from his camp. Above all, they were to prevent a general rising of Tories, chiefly by preventing armed bodies from joining the main British army.

The attacking force was put across the swift Dan in Carrington's boats on Feb. 18, without incident, and within a few hours the daredevil cavalrymen on fine Virginia horses were watching the enemy's rear guard. By nightfall the band lay in hidden camp near the road leading from the upper crossings of the Haw River to Hillsboro. Lee sent horsemen in both directions along this road to explore the country.

About dark there was a surprise visitor: Nathanael Greene, who had ridden out with a small party of Washington's horsemen, leaving the main army in camp north of the Dan. Greene spent several hours with Lee and Pickens in review of his plan:

He would cross the Dan in force within a few days and march to upper North Carolina. He would not come close enough to provide protection for the advance force, which must use caution and defend itself. He urged special vigilance and once more stressed the importance of keeping Tory reinforcements from Cornwallis.

Late in the night Greene borrowed a blanket from Pickens and slept by a campfire. When he woke at dawn, there was a report from riders who had penetrated toward the Haw: Banastre Tarleton had passed in that direction from Hillsboro with infantry, cavalry, and two small cannon. His strength was unknown, but he was said to be scouting for Tory parties, which he would escort to Cornwallis. When Lee and Pickens had made plans to trap Tarleton, Greene returned to his army.

Lee and Pickens marched hard all day and at dusk were within seven miles of the Haw, which the British were ready to cross. Scouts found but one person on the road, a boy who reported that the British were by the river. The enemy strength was now estimated at 400 infantry and a strong party of cavalry, besides the two guns. (Tarleton's orders had sent him out with 200 cavalry, 150 of Colonel Webster's infantry, and 100 Yagers "to give countenance to the friends of government in that district.")

On the following morning Lee and Pickens crossed the Haw and found the plain trail of the enemy. Lee said:

Guides became unnecessary now; for the British detachment had plundered all the houses on the road, known, as they were, to be the property of patriots, and symbols of devastation marked their steps. The men having all fled, none but women could be seen.

Roadside gossip told Lee that the British would not march far beyond the Haw, since the redcoats said they would be only a few days outside Hillsboro. There were reports that the Loyalists between the Deep and Haw Rivers were gathering, and that Tarleton was to escort them to camp.

A scout came back with word that Tarleton had camped three miles away at noon, his horses unsaddled, and few pickets posted. The Americans planned an attack with Lee and his Legion infantry in the lead and dragoons on the flank. The Maryland infantry was close behind, ready to charge the enemy cannon with bayonets if the opportunity arose. The scout led them to the farm where Tarleton had been, but the camp was gone. A galloping charge by dragoons captured two

British supply officers, who went along as prisoners. Tarleton was now six miles ahead, and Lee, cursing at the missed opportunity of flushing the enemy in a vulnerable position, pushed his force ahead. He forced the captured officers to ride at the front, adding to the impression that this was Tarleton's column—for both Legion commands wore green coats. Lee promised the captives instant death if they made a false move during the approach toward the enemy.

Banastre Tarleton's carelessness in movements and making camp was unaccountable. He had left Hillsboro at full speed, in chase of a bold American company which had ambushed and destroyed a picket at Hart's Mill, where the army was grinding cornmeal on the Eno River.

The attack was made by Capt. Joseph Graham, the boy cavalryman who had fought at Cowan's Ford. Graham had taken twenty of his mounted men and about as many picked infantrymen, and after a night march fell upon the enemy outpost. Graham had spied on the twenty-nine British soldiers at the mill, then divided his party in two. Half his force attacked over open ground in front of the mill, and the rest came from the rear. Nine British were killed or wounded and nineteen captured; the young lieutenant who commanded hid in the mill until the shooting stopped. The scene was only half a mile outside Hillsboro, and the firing quickly brought British cavalry patrols to the rescue; Graham fled, and Tarleton moved westward in his track, assigned to the larger purpose of bringing in a Tory band.

The Tory leader of the area was Dr. John Pyle, now called Colonel, the patriarch of a large family of Loyalists between the Deep and Haw Rivers. For several days volunteers had been assembling at his home, until there were, about Feb.

20, some 400 men. Tarleton tried to hurry them into his camp and then to Hillsboro, but the Tories would not be rushed.

Tarleton wrote: "Colonel Pyle and . . . his followers, being all equally ignorant of the customs of war, had not complied with the orders they received, and though forewarned of their danger, thought fit to pay visits to their kindred and acquaintance before they repaired to the British camp. Inspired by whiskey and the novelty of their situation, they unfortunately prolonged their excursions."

The country west of the upper Haw River, the future Alamance County of North Carolina, was largely a wilderness through which the great road ran from Hillsboro to Salisbury. Near the river was a barren country of haw and locust, gum and scrub oaks. Canebrakes and alder thickets screened the river and its myriad tributaries. Through this country, halting frequently at cabins to drink to the health of King George, Pyle and his Tories moved toward the camp of Tarleton.

Pyle sent two young riders in advance to find the British cavalryman; they ran into Lee's vanguard, who convinced them that they were among friends. The boy soldiers said they were seeking Tarleton, and were ready to lead up Pyle and his 400 men, who were in the road just ahead. They were sent back to Harry Lee, so deceived that they addressed the Virginia horseman as Colonel Tarleton and spoke with enthusiasm of the Tory rising in the region.

Lee ordered Pickens to bring his riflemen up on the left flank in an attempt to surround the Tory band and then sent the two confused boys to the front. Lee asked them to present Tarleton's congratulations to Colonel Pyle and to instruct him to halt his men on the roadside while the column passed through. Lee explained that the troops were tired and must reach their campsite for the night before the accursed Americans came upon them. The boys disappeared on the road, which now led through dense woodlands.

One of the young Tories returned with word that Pyle was waiting at the roadside, as ordered, the men drawn up on the right-hand side. The column approached the mounted Tories and without pause the Virginia cavalrymen filed along the road until the two bands were parallel, near enough for the riders to touch each other. Pyle's men were unsuspecting, their muskets and rifles over their shoulders, looking with curiosity at the troops they took to be Tarleton's famed Legion.

Harry Lee acted out the deception to the end. He passed to the head of his column, nodding to the Tories, passing an occasional compliment on their soldierly appearance. He rode up to Pyle and shook hands. Lee later recalled that his intention was to tell Pyle that he was surrounded and at his mercy, and that he should surrender the band. Firing broke out at the end of the column as the leaders met.

It appeared to Lee that Tories had caught sight of the approaching militia of Pickens, who were no longer hidden, and saw from the green twigs in their hats that they were Whigs. The enemy then began to fire.

Witnesses nearer the scene of the opening shots recalled that the mounted militia at the rear of Lee's column, ignorant of the battle plan, saw the red cloth strips in the hats of the Tories and became alarmed. Captain Joseph Eggleston, commander of these riders, shouted to a Tory at the roadside in an attempt to allay the fears of his men:

"Who do you fight for?"

"For the King!"

Eggleston cut the Tory on the head with a saber, and the

militia charged the Tories, swinging blades and firing their weapons.

The militia rushed in from the woodlands, and Lee's horsemen, strung out in perfect position, sabered the unprepared enemy so swiftly that, by Lee's own estimate, ninety were killed and most of the others wounded. Some escaped by riding recklessly through the deep, tangled woods.

Some of the Tories still thought there was a ghastly error and many shouted: "You're killing your own men!" "We're friends of His Majesty!" "Hurrah for King George!"

Lee heard the shouts of assurance and also cries for mercy, but the affair was out of control: "No expostulation could be admitted in a conjuncture so critical," he said.

A band of about a dozen Tories, braver than the rest, clung together for defense and shot in all directions, but their wild firing caused only one casualty, a wounded horse shot as the cavalry of Lee rode them down. The American militia hacked at the enemy so fiercely that many of the homemade swords were bent or broken.

Lee reported no men killed or wounded. The remnant of the Tories fled, and Colonel Pyle, who had several wounds, escaped by hiding in a small pond near the site, according to tradition. He survived his wounds, at any rate, and, when later captured, was pardoned for his kind treatment of American wounded on other fields. John Pyle, Jr., was also wounded in this affair.

Soon after the slaughter Capt. Conway Oldham, a fine field officer who had been disciplined earlier for insubordination, arrived with a band of infantry. In the new party were some Catawba Indian allies, and these men, fired by sight of the wounded, fell upon the victims before they could be halted, and speared six or eight of the Tories. Tales of atrocities spread.

The writer Stedman, traveling with Cornwallis, wrote of this action:

> They called out for quarter, but no quarter was granted; and between two and three hundred of them were inhumanly butchered while in the act of begging for mercy. Humanity shudders at . . . so foul a massacre.

Lee later replied:

> It was not foul, and was unintentional. . . . The fire commenced upon us, and self-preservation commanded the limited destruction which ensued. Only ninety of the loyalists were killed . . . and less than ninety could not have been spared from the close condition of the dragoons, and the necessity of crushing resistance instantly.

Lee added that, if he had intended a massacre, he could have ordered pursuit and killed the last of the band; instead, he resumed his march.

Tarleton lay in camp a mile away from this action, undisturbed. The sound of the skirmish did not carry to him, and he was unaware of it until wounded survivors entered his camp with complaints of the cruelty of Tarleton's dragoons. The cavalryman soon learned the truth of Lee's deception and got details of the fight. He sent assistance to the wounded men; patrols went out in the dark on the trail of the Americans. Near midnight on Feb. 25, a dispatch from Cornwallis ordered Tarleton back to Hillsboro.

Lee and Pickens had halted at dusk, convinced that they should not attack Tarleton's camp at the late hour, since the troops were worn with the day's work. During the night they were joined by 300 hardened riflemen, commanded by Col.

John Preston, of Montgomery County, Virginia. At daybreak the band went on the trail of the retreating Tarleton, but turned back at the crossing of the Haw River.

Nathanael Greene took his main army back across the Dan into North Carolina on Feb. 23, two days before Lee butchered the band of Pyle. The Quaker now had 2,000 new Virginia militia, most of them well-armed, and 1,000 more had been promised. Stevens had 700 men, Col. William Campbell had brought 600 mountain riflemen, and other veterans sent word that they were on the way.

Greene still turned away men without guns—and when he ordered the dismounting of hundreds of men who had brought their horses, desertions became common once more. Militia, even the frontier riflemen, resented the loss of their horses, which robbed them of a means of immediate retreat; Greene was firm, realizing that he could not feed so many animals.

He moved into the overgrown country of the upper Haw River, whose three chief tributaries were, from north to south, Troublesome Creek, Reedy Fork Creek, and Alamance Creek.

Two days after Greene recrossed the Dan, Cornwallis moved westward from Hillsboro and camped on Alamance Creek at the pungently named Stinking Quarter. Greene thrust the light corps of Otho Williams before him once more, calling Lee and Pickens to join the screen; Cornwallis was effectively blinded as to the movements of the main army. The Quaker opened a delicate and dangerous phase of the campaign. His superior strength was largely an illusion because of the undependable militia; the danger of being caught against the broad Dan was almost as great as ever. He set out to confuse Cornwallis.

The army was never more than forty-eight hours in one camp and often moved daily. This was not only from fear of enemy attack. Colonel Davie, the genius of supply, must collect provisions in advance of every move—yet he could not establish depots along a route which would betray plans to the enemy. Every night from eleven o'clock to midnight Davie talked with Greene while other officers slept. They spread maps, talked of the enemy's position and probable movements, and selected new spots for supply posts. Davie remembered it: "The General, tracing the direction on the map with his finger, would observe if the Enemy move in this direction, I must take a position there, can subsistence be procured."

As the army moved, the small trains of supplies moved too. Civilians, many of them Tories, were baffled by the marching and countermarching. The country seemed to be full of American troops. The Tory cause in the neighborhood became more sickly each day.

Greene had risked his advance in order to stop the recruiting of Tories in North Carolina, which he thought would prove fatal if allowed to proceed unchecked. Since the destruction of Pyle's band he was much encouraged. He had crossed the Dan without sufficient supplies, especially of ammunition, which had been sent across the Staunton River in Virginia for safekeeping. But, as he wrote to Congress, he felt that "it was best to put on a good face, and make the most of appearances."

It was the enemy himself who did most to improve those appearances, for Cornwallis and his troops seemed to alienate both friends and foes at every turn.

Tories now refused to spy for Cornwallis, for they were

frightened by the fate of Pyle and outraged by the behavior of redcoats. Since he could get no information through the usual channels, Cornwallis pushed Tarleton ahead of him in the direction of Deep River in an effort to puzzle out the intentions of Greene.

British plundering continued even here, in the country where Tories were said to be most numerous. His Lordship investigated and found that the women with his army were "the most infamous looters." He ordered all women searched, their baggage inspected, and all suspicious articles burned. He held frequent roll calls for his men and forced the women to attend, standing in rear of the files. Men who were absent were treated as deserters, and women who were absent were whipped and drummed out of camp. All women were required to witness punishments, from floggings to executions. Even this did not halt depredations, and the country people became more hostile to the invaders.

Greene sent raiding parties against Tarleton by day and night, and the British detachment on Deep River became more nervous. One day when a Tory band approached the English camp, ready to enlist, a sentry fired on it. Tarleton's dragoons dashed out at the sound and without waiting for an explanation rode down the visitors, killing or wounding those who could not flee into the woods. When Tarleton discovered the error, he tried to find the survivors, but none could be found.

On the following night a patrol of William Washington's cavalry caught a party of twenty-five Tories as they were driving cattle to the British troops. Twenty-three of the herders were killed, and the beeves went astray.

The few Tories who had recently joined Cornwallis began to desert after a few days of such fighting and returned to their homes. Many went to Greene's camp to volunteer—and by now British regulars were also deserting to the Americans. Cornwallis tried to stem the tide by offering a reward of two guineas to the Tories for every deserter returned to camp. His Lordship also urged his soldiers to be more civil to the native Tories, on the ground that they were as loyal to the King's cause as any Englishmen under arms.

During early March, as this game was played out, Greene moved back and forth, first coming forward as if to join Otho Williams, who sometimes camped within three miles of Cornwallis, then falling back as far as High Rock Ford on Troublesome Creek, as if he would retreat from the theater. Cornwallis concluded that Greene would not dare attack until he had great superiority in numbers. His Lordship determined that he would press the issue himself with his whole force, since Tarleton's Legion did not seem to be effective in this kind of warfare.

On Mar. 2, while probing enemy lines at Clapp's Mill on Alamance Creek, Tarleton fell into a trap set by Harry Lee, whose Legion was reinforced with militia and the party of Catawba Indians. The Americans lay in ambush along a rail fence, with cavalry on either flank, and their first fire drove Tarleton back in confusion. When the British re-formed and charged, the Indians fled, though the British fired high, the bullets whistling harmlessly through the trees overhead. The falling of limbs frightened Lee's militia, however, and it retreated after the Indians. Lee pulled off his Legion in small parties, sending them into many roads and trails to confuse pursuit. There were few casualties despite the rather large numbers engaged. Tarleton reported one officer and twenty men dead or wounded; Lee lost eight men.

This sparring continued for several days, broken only by a conference between the armies in which an exchange of prisoners was arranged.

On Mar. 6 Cornwallis made a swift thrust at his enemies. Scouts told him that Otho Williams's light corps was in camp near his own position and that Greene with the main army was some miles away across the Haw River. Williams seemed to have gone into camp carelessly, the strength of his forces depleted by their being posted on separate plantations in order to make subsistence easier. His Lordship determined to attack Williams, drive him back on the main army, and by investing the final position bring Greene to battle and force the issue of the dragging campaign.

The British moved at 3 A.M., in fog hanging so densely over the swampy thickets that the column was within a mile of Williams before it was discovered. Williams had also chosen this morning for attack—a raid on a small British outpost at a mill in his front—and an officer leading this raid discovered that the British were in motion. Even so, the Americans had a close call.

The left position of Williams's force was held by the mountain riflemen of Colonel Campbell, who had come in to relieve Andrew Pickens and his weary militia. The mountaineers, as informal in camp routine as on the battlefield, neglected their sentries, and there was firing by the oncoming enemy before the riflemen were awake. Lieutenant Colonel Webster's redcoat infantry was in close range. The Americans recovered nimbly.

Williams threw a force of riflemen and cavalry across Reedy Fork Creek to the vicinity of Wetzell's Mill; he soon learned from a scout that the British main body was marching toward the same objective. Williams narrowly won the race and temporarily escaped danger, blocking Cornwallis in his effort to march to the left flank of the American position. Williams sent many small parties to snipe at the British in the overgrown woodlands, but the big column could not be turned aside. The vanguard of Webster's infantry and Tarleton's cavalry pushed so rapidly that the American rear guard was often swept back along the flanks and was pressed to keep up. This chase went on for about ten miles with such vigor that Williams barely managed to cross Reedy Fork Creek by the ford at Wetzell's Mill.

Williams placed militia from the Carolinas, Virginia, and Georgia on the south bank of the stream to give covering fire while the main body crossed. Lee's horsemen were on the flanks of this rear guard, supported by a few riders of William Washington. The little army splashed through the water to the north bank, forming in defensive position along wooded hills overlooking the creek, while the rear guard held off the enemy. Firing was so hot that the British fell back in confusion, re-formed and came on again, and were once more forced back. The riflemen and the reckless cavalrymen held on until Williams was safely across the ford, then crossed themselves before the British could recover. Many of the militia did not halt in the defensive positions.

Cornwallis formed a storming party under Colonel Webster to force the ford. British infantry spread along the stream and, since it was longer than the American line, soon poured a deadly fire into one flank of Williams's men. This did not lessen the rifle fire upon the British party at the ford. Two British cannon had come up, and roared across the stream, their outrageous bellowing echoing for miles through the swamp country, frightening civilians and militia alike. Under their fire Webster moved into the water, riding down a steep slope in the road above the stream. Harry Lee watched from across the creek: "A field officer rode up, and in a loud voice addressed his soldiers, then rushed down the hill at their head, and plunged into the water, our fire pouring upon him."

Lee had placed twenty-five picked mountain riflemen in a cabin nearby, under orders to take no part in a general engagement but to be ready for assigned targets. He now ordered them to kill Webster, who was within close range. The Kings Mountain veterans fired through cracks in the logs where mud chinking had fallen out. Lee followed anxiously:

"The stream being deep, and the bottom rugged, he advanced slowly, his soldiers on each side of him, and apparently some of them holding his stirrup leathers. This select party discharged their rifles at him, one by one, each man sure of knocking him over; and having reloaded, eight or nine of them emptied their guns a second time. Strange to tell, himself and horse were untouched; and having crossed the creek, he soon formed his troops and advanced upon us."

Lee was astonished at the failure of the riflemen, for he had often seen them in camp, at great range, shooting several holes in an apple held on a ramrod by a companion—yet with about thirty-two shots they had missed horse and rider at point-blank range.

The American light corps was now in its greatest danger, for the enemy soon crossed the creek and formed ranks with Tarleton's cavalry on the right, near the road over which Williams must escape. One wing of the British infantry had overrun a hill which overlooked the American position. Lee took several prisoners in the melee, but the British were too strong. Only his cavalry, galloping back and forth before Williams's infantrymen, enabled the main body to reach the route of retreat. Lee

fell back slowly, still screening the detachment; bands of infantry hung on the British flanks in the thick woodlands, but
the chase continued five miles farther before Cornwallis gave
up. Greene's army, undisturbed, was still on the north side of
the Haw. Williams now got a message that the Quaker would
remain there, keeping open his communications and welcoming the incoming militia bands. Williams was ordered to return to headquarters.

Casualties of the skirmish, as usual, were something of a
mystery. Tarleton set the American loss at 100 dead and
wounded; Williams claimed that his own loss was slight, and
that deserters reported at least 100 British casualties.

Greene's most serious loss was in militia. The riflemen
from South Carolina and Georgia complained that they had
been discriminated against and were needlessly exposed on
the bank of the river to screen the passage of the regulars.
They intended to go home at once. Williams and other officers
thought that it was the noisy cannon which had cooled the
patriotism of the militia, but only Colonel Pickens could deal
with the irate volunteers.

Pickens returned from Greene's headquarters, where he
had been conferring with Governor John Rutledge, to find
these men waiting for him—only to know if he intended to
go home with them. Pickens persuaded them to wait until he
had talked with Greene and at headquarters got permission
to go with them to South Carolina, where he was directed to
form a core of resistance to the British force of occupation.
Pickens was also assured by Greene that he would bring the
entire army to South Carolina when he had dealt with Cornwallis—when he had the chance "to break this fellow's leg."

The militia dispute brought a squabble in the American
command, for Williams declined to command a screening

force of a different composition, and in compromise Greene shielded his main group with two parties of light troops, one operating on each flank. These parties of regular cavalry and militia infantry were commanded by William Washington and Harry Lee, an arrangement which seemed to satisfy all officers concerned.

Governor Rutledge left camp as a diplomat at the urging of Greene, riding off to visit the governors of North Carolina, Virginia, and Maryland and the Congress in Philadelphia, to plead for more men and supplies. Militia drifted in and out daily, in such waves that neither Greene's staff nor Cornwallis's spies could fix the strength of the American army. The men who came in great numbers with the return of the army to North Carolina soon deserted, once they experienced the rigors of camp life. Food and supplies had become scarcer by the day as the armies picked the countryside clean.

Greene had come down from Virginia under the lightest possible marching order. There were few wagons, and those were loaded with the bare necessities of the army. The only tents were those brought to cover the ammunition in the event of rain.

The affair at Wetzell's Mill convinced Greene that he was not yet ready to meet Cornwallis in open battle; the militia had behaved much as he expected; the enemy had been able to surprise the most veteran and alert of his light troops; the natural advantage of the native defenders in the tangled wilderness country had been offset by the vigor of the British attack.

The Quaker became more popular with his men through this phase of maneuvers. They saw that he shared the scanty food they ate—and more than once was forced to send men to borrow from the campfires of private soldiers. He seemed to be the last man in camp to go to bed, and the first to rise. He made constant patrols of the sentry posts, on foot and often alone, to see that the sentries were alert. He knew that Cornwallis favored early morning attacks, and now, in the second week of March, as he shifted slowly westward along the Haw River, frequently moving his camp, he kept such a watch as might be expected of a captain of cavalry.

Early one morning as he walked the rounds, the Quaker came upon Col. John Greene, who was snoring loudly. He shook the Colonel awake: "How can you sleep so soundly, with the enemy so near?"

The Colonel stared sleepily: "Why, General, I knew you were awake." The Quaker remembered it as the greatest compliment ever paid him.

There was also his superior cavalry to protect him, and he gave free rein to the talented Virginians, Lee and Washington; they made few errors. Lee was especially adept at holding a tantalizing screen of troopers just in front of Cornwallis, the riders maneuvering like mounted dervishes along the screened roads, cutting off British scouts, threatening outposts, and gathering information for Greene. Lee was confident that the British cavalry was no match for him, either in men or horses:

"No country in the world affords better riders than the United States, especially the States south of Pennsylvania. The boys from seven years of age begin to mount horses; riding without saddles, and often in the fields. . . . They go to mill on horseback, and perform all the other small domestic services mounted. They become so completely versed in the art of riding by the time they reach puberty, as to equal the most expert horsemen anywhere."

Since the Americans usually had first choice of the horses to be found in the countryside, their mounts were also superior. Lee, at least, was convinced that "Lord Cornwallis well knew the superiority of our horse, feeling it daily in the counteraction of his efforts." When Cornwallis withdrew slightly to the south and west, going into camp at Bell's Mills on the Deep River, Lee attributed the move to British frustration in the face of superior cavalry.

Greene continued to move westward along the Haw, which ran roughly parallel to the Deep. He settled for a few days at High Rock Ford, a main passage on the north-south road which led through Guilford Courthouse. The armies were about twenty miles apart.

On Mar. 10 the Quaker began to change his mind about his prospects. On that day he wrote to Thomas Jefferson, as if in reply to critics of his Fabian campaign of retreat:

> I have been obliged to practice that by finesse which I dared not attempt by force. I know the people have been in anxious suspense, waiting the event of a general action; but be the consequence of censure what it may, nothing shall hurry me into a measure that is not suggested by prudence or connects not with it the interest of the southern department.

In the night, the first arrival of new troops gave Greene new hope. In the next two days two brigades of North Carolina militia were led in by Generals John Butler and Thomas Eaton. General Robert Lawson, who had been inspired by Daniel Morgan, arrived with more than 1,000 Virginia militia, so that General Stevens now commanded at least 1,700 men from his State. Baron von Steuben had sent down 530 Virginia Continentals, commanded by Lt. Col. Richard Campbell. The western riflemen under the frontier colonels, Charles Lynch, Hugh Crocket, and William Campbell, were at least 400 strong.

Greene now had more than 4,200 men, so that almost overnight he outnumbered Cornwallis so considerably that he could consider giving battle. The British force was estimated at from 2,000 to 2,400 men, all of them dependable veterans under superb discipline.

Greene's staff did not keep the secret well, and there was soon campfire gossip of the coming battle. On Mar. 11 and 12 Lee skirmished with the enemy, taking about twenty prisoners in the two days. One of Lawson's Virginia militia officers, St. George Tucker of Williamsburg, wrote his wife on Mar. 13:

> We marched yesterday to look for Lord Cornwallis who probably march'd a different rout because he did not choose to fight us. We are now strong enough, I am in hopes, to cope with him. . . . I should conclude that we had about six thousand Men, of which I believe fifteen hundred are regulars. . . . We dined with General Greene the Day we came to camp. He has an Aspect which commands respect—something of the Washington about him.

On Mar. 14, the day Greene finally decided to go into battle, Tucker wrote from High Rock Ford on Troublesome Creek:

> We joined Gen. Greene last night and are this Moment marching to attack Lord Cornwallis with a Force which I am in hopes is full able to cope with him. . . .

The armies were about ten or fifteen miles apart on this day. Sergeant Seymour of the Delaware regiment noted in his journal that they had marched 190 miles in about seven days, and estimated that they had not been more than ten or twelve miles from Guilford Courthouse in all of that time. He sketched the region:

> This part of the country is very thickly inhabited; the land indeed is not productive, yielding corn and some grain.

Along the Haw River you may see some good settlements, especially the Haw Fields, which abound . . . with fine corn fields, wheat, rye, oats and barley. The inhabitants here and about Guilford Courthouse are chiefly Irish, being very courteous, humane and affable to strangers. . . .

The country nearer Guilford Courthouse was wilder, cut by ravines in the rolling timbered hills, its dense forests overgrown by mountains of peavines which now lay brown and dormant. It had once been buffalo country.

Greene's army arrived at the isolated village in the late afternoon on Mar. 14, waiting for the enemy. The men went into camp around the courthouse.

Cornwallis once thought he might circle the entire American army to seize the fords of the Dan in its rear, but it was only a dream, "the extreme difficulty of subsisting my troops in that exhausted country putting it out of my power to force them." He fell back first to Bell's Mills on the Deep River, then moved slightly toward the American position and camped at plantations on North and South Buffalo Creeks, from which he sent out foragers. Lee did not hesitate; almost every party leaving the British camp was attacked.

Cornwallis had moved deliberately to force a battle. He had marched to Bell's Mills in hopes of protecting his supply route to Cross Creek, far down on the Cape Fear River, then gave up that position to avoid giving Greene the chance of choosing the ground for an attack.

The British force was shrinking steadily, and, despite the claim that he lost but 101 men in his campaign through North Carolina, Cornwallis had a loss of 227 men from his rolls in February alone. The supply of the troops was becoming desperate, and much of the army's time was spent in finding leather for shoes. His Lordship was forced to move to new ground in an effort to feed and clothe the men; he also hoped to find Greene in more open country. The British moved a few miles westward, toward a Quaker meetinghouse between the forks of the Deep River. He camped there on Mar. 13. On the next day, he had news that Greene was moving toward him and had reached Guilford Courthouse, some twelve miles distant. The American strength was reported at 7,000 men. Cornwallis did not hesitate; he planned battle the following day and sent back most of his remaining baggage to safety down the Deep River.

It was on Mar. 13 that a party of Lee's raiding dragoons, casting about Bell's Mills, found the position abandoned; the British had left the plantations on the Buffalo Creeks, as well. The leader of this scouting party followed the route of the British baggage, which went astray over the wrong road, and sent a messenger to Lee.

The cavalryman got the news at 11 P.M., but he put two companies of infantry and two troops of cavalry on the road, with guides riding ahead. He floundered through most of the night, with the confused guides lost in the darkness, often leading the party in false directions. Lee did not forget this outing:

> It was now three o'clock, as well as we could make out the time by feeling the hour and minute-hands of our watches. Again we mounted, and again moved as our guides directed; more and more bewildered, and more and more distressed; persevering, and yet in vain. . . .

At dawn, by studying the moss on tree trunks, his guides found their position, but it was too late to attack the British baggage, which had spent the night only two miles away. The enemy wagons escaped under a heavy guard of infantry sent by Cornwallis, and Lee turned back toward the army "much mortified." He soon met a party of Campbell's riflemen and got orders from Greene to report to headquarters at Guilford Courthouse. It was now about noon on Mar. 14. The night of floundering in the strange woodlands was Lee's preparation for battle.

Guilford Courthouse
March 15, 1781

THE FIRST RIDER CAME POUNDING IN TO HARRY LEE AT TWO in the morning, a little breathless, with a report from the advance scouting party of Legion cavalry:

Lieutenant Heard had taken them near the British camp, as ordered—but there was now movement. A large body of enemy cavalry was riding in the direction of Guilford Courthouse. They had been near a Quaker meetinghouse an hour ago—perhaps six miles away, on this same great road leading to Salisbury.

Lee was posted in the woodlands beside the road two or three miles to the west of Greene and the main army. He got reports from Heard every half-hour, as he had ordered. The riders came in through the night:

The enemy was coming on, slowly, now more horsemen than before.

Heard had tried to circle down the enemy flank but was cut off by scouting parties on every trail.

Late in the night, there was the rumble of heavy wheels. Big guns. The whole enemy army was in motion.

Lee sent word back to Greene and was ordered to take his force westward and investigate the enemy. Lee went in the dark road with his Virginia cavalrymen, an infantry force on his left and riflemen on his right. Within two miles he met the squad of Lieutenant Heard, trotting slowly. Heard reported that the enemy was close behind, advancing with caution. Lee devised a retreat which became an ambush.

His infantry and riflemen were now some distance in his rear; he ordered the cavalry to wheel and move back to the east, to get within reach of their support and approach Greene's army before risking too much.

The roadway was narrow and winding, bordered by high fences which hid all but the helmets of the mounted troopers. Lee sent back the rear troop, under Capt. John Rudolph; it left at a gallop. Capt. Joseph Eggleston took off the center troop. Lee remained with Captain Armstrong and a single troop. The enemy crowded on the rear, flailing with sabers, and, when they were unable to move the Virginians, fired a few rounds with pistols.

Lee abruptly ordered a charge, and the dragoons whirled and shattered the leading section of Tarleton's men, forcing them off their smaller, inferior horses, taking prisoners and killing several men without a loss. The British fled out of the road and cross-country toward their main army, just as gray dawn broke.

Lee followed by another road, hoping to cut off Tarleton from Cornwallis, but when he approached a nearby Quaker meetinghouse at New Garden, he was fired upon by British infantry—the Brigade of Guards. Lee's horse was frightened by the volley, or the glittering of British arms, and threw his rider. Lee mounted another horse and called to his men to

retreat, but the infantry of the Legion caught up with him
at that moment and fired on the Guards. Campbell's riflemen
also fired from the protection of trees, and for almost half
an hour the parties skirmished about the church. Cornwallis
ended it by sending up the Welsh Fusileers, and Lee retreated
with his column.

Lee reported that the British had many more killed and
wounded than he did, including a captain of the Guards killed
(Goodrick) and Tarleton, who was shot in the hand with a
musket ball. An infantry lieutenant of the Legion, one Snow-
den, was left wounded on this field. Tarleton reported between twenty and thirty men killed or wounded.

Lee's party trailed back the few miles along the great
road to Guilford Courthouse, reported to Greene, and were
stationed on the left flank of the front line. It was mid-
morning. Greene put the army into final position.

Guilford Courthouse stood in a small clearing in the
wilderness, at the edge of the Salisbury road. The undulating
ground fell away from it westward, along this road, to the
valley of Little Horsepen Creek, half a mile away. Most of
the neighborhood was clothed in timber, except for fields
around the courthouse, and cornfields beside the road on the
slope above Little Horsepen. There were few dwellings, one
of them the log cabin of a Quaker farmer, Joseph Hoskins,
which stood on the south side of the road at the western edge
of a cornfield.

Between this cabin and the courthouse Nathanael Greene
made his stand. He had in mind the battle plan of Daniel
Morgan, and the ground was familiar to him.

In the first line, on the eastern edge of the Hoskins corn
fields, he placed the North Carolina militia, General Eaton on

the left and General Butler on the right. The line spraddled
the road, stretching for almost half a mile when flank parties
had been added. The center of the line was lightly protected
by a rail fence, from which the militia of nearby counties
looked down across the wet red fields, deep in mud and yet
unploughed for the season. Beyond lay only the cabin of
Hoskins and the great road, which fell out of sight as it
forded Little Horsepen in the dense woodland.

Greene anchored the far right of this line with the riflemen of Colonel Lynch and with Kirkwood and his Delaware
troops—and even beyond this a strong party of William
Washington's troopers. The opposite side, hidden by woodlands, was flanked by the riflemen of Campbell and Harry
Lee's cavalry.

Greene spoke to the militiamen: If they would fire two
rounds, they might retire. That would be their contribution
to victory. He neglected to say how far they should retire.

Three hundred yards to the rear of this line, on a slight
knoll covered by large trees, the Quaker formed a line of the
Virginia militia, these men more veteran, with a liberal sprinkling of old Continental soldiers who had returned with
Lawson and Stevens. Their line was about half as long as that
of the North Carolinians, with another important difference:
Edward Stevens had been humiliated by the flight of his men
at the battle of Camden and by their insistence upon returning home when the army needed them so badly. At the
rear of his line he placed forty picked marksmen, with
orders to shoot down any man who fled from the British
today. The order was made plain to all the troops on both
sides of the road. Stevens commanded on the right of this line
and Lawson on the left. There were no flanking parties.

Some 500 yards farther eastward, not far from the courthouse, Greene placed his crack troops, the Continentals from Maryland and Virginia. They lay in two wings, in the form of a broad V, to the north of the great road. Their hillside position overlooked a shallow, open ravine through which flowed a wet-weather stream.

General Huger commanded the right segment of this line, made up of the Virginians of Colonels John Greene and Samuel Hawes. The left segment, nearest the road, was commanded by Col. Otho Williams, two Maryland regiments under Colonels Benjamin Ford and John Gunby. Gunby's regiment was the most experienced in the army, the survivors of all the fighting since Camden; Ford's men had lately joined as recruits. The officers of both Maryland regiments were skilled veterans.

In the center of this final line were two cannon. Greene placed two more cannon in advance, before the first line in the roadway.

There was less than half a mile between his first and third lines. Each line seemed to be firmly anchored, with riflemen and cavalry, or attached to ravines and other natural obstacles in deep woods. The landscape was designed to break up the customary charge of the British infantry. In the rear, routes of retreat were open, if necessary. The great road led straight east, and a lesser road ran northward past the courthouse, toward the swamps around Reedy Fork. Greene had placed every man in line and was without reserves. The enemy would be outnumbered here and must commit his entire force to avoid being outflanked. The men of the army ate near noon, where they lay, and waited. It had been some hours since the first gunfire from the distance where Lee's men had fought.

The Quaker made a brief speech to the men of the front

line, reminding them of their duty and their chance to win their liberty, but he was not an inspiring speaker, and the men appeared to be unmoved. Not long afterward Harry Lee passed down the line on his sweat-stained horse, shouting dramatically, exhorting them to stand firm and have no fear of the British: "I have whipped them three times this morning, and can do it again."

One cavalryman, a Quaker by the name of Peter Rife, overheard that morning one of Greene's aides who brought Lee an order to take command of the left flank of the front line. Rife reported that Lee refused: "Tell General Greene that I cannot and will not. Both my men and my horses are run down." Lee had ridden twenty-five or thirty miles, fought three skirmishes, and returned to the main army—all without rest from the exertions of the previous night, when he had been out on his chase of the enemy's baggage.

It was almost 1:30 P.M. when the first of the enemy appeared. Greene had waited in the front line, at the two six-pounders in the roadway, with Lieutenant Singleton of the artillery. The road was clear before them, falling for about 400 yards to the small stream, then climbing between huge trees, narrow ruts mounting the far slope. The creek flowed across the road at the bottom of this valley.

The British column was strikingly colorful as it came over and down the hill, the column moving as precisely as the rough slope would allow. Horsemen led, with infantry close behind. The advance halted at sight of the American guns in the road above, and after a few moments an officer came into sight and studied Greene's position with a glass. Cornwallis, it was assumed.

Greene ordered Singleton to open fire, and for a few

rounds the guns plunged and shot fell along the distant hill-side—to little effect. British guns came into sight at a rapid trot, were unlimbered on the creek bank, and began a return of fire. Limbs toppled from trees over the American first line. One or two men on the right flank, in Butler's line, were killed. On the left, a private by the name of Pinkerton, who was leaning forward on one knee, was killed by a shot which plunged down his back, tearing out his spine. Almost all of Singleton's artillery horses, tied at the roadside, were killed by the cannon shot.

Under cover of the growing smoke pall in the creek bottom the British came forward, and men in the first line saw them turning to each side of the road, in formation. Singleton called up more horses and carried his guns to the rear. There was a time of silence.

Cornwallis saw the obvious: The road cutting the center of the American position was the only clear passage, and that was covered by the enemy muskets and rifles. The trees appeared to be less dense on his left, and he determined to put his major force on that side. The depth of the wet fields and the density of the timber would keep the artillery on the road, and perhaps the cavalry as well.

The British veterans worked flawlessly. Just short of the Hoskins cabin they left the road. To the right the Germans, the Bose Regiment, and the 71st Highlanders formed lines, Major General Leslie commanding. Just to their rear, as a temporary reserve, was the First Battalion of the Guards. Officers called commands, and these units quickly fell into files in the yard of the Hoskins house, the cornfield opening ahead of them.

On the north of the road, on the British left flank, Corn-wallis placed the bulk of his strength. The Thirty-third and

Twenty-third Regiments were in the front line under Lieutenant Colonel Webster, with the Yagers and Light Infantry of the Guard behind them, and a reserve of the Guards composed of the Grenadiers and the Second Battalion. Brigadier General O'Hara was in command on this flank.

The cannon kept up their fire as the redcoat lines formed, and some sniper fire came from the American front; a Lieutenant O'Hara, an artilleryman, was killed, the first British casualty of the afternoon.

The militia was frightened by the deliberate pace of the British infantry; the men behind the rail fence, most of whom had never seen a battle, lay and listened to the loading and ramming of the British muskets and the barked orders of the officers. The enemy files came into the open, across the muddy cornfields, almost without a sound. Some militiamen left the line and went rearward, but most of them held to their places until, when the British were within about forty paces, a volley was fired from the front line.

On the British right this was disastrous. Captain Dugald Stuart of the 71st said: "We received a very deadly fire, from the Irish line of the American army, composed of their marksmen lying on the ground behind a rail fence. One half of the Highlanders dropped on that spot, there ought to be a pretty large tumulus where our men were buried."

In this front, holding firm as more of the militia ran away, was the company of Capt. Arthur Forbis of Alamance. Forbis was said to have fired the first shot at the enemy in the cornfield and to have brought down an officer. Most of his company was killed or wounded, and Forbis lay, fatally wounded, for some time after the battle.

The British halted under the fire and, when they were near the rail fence, raised their muskets and fired a volley;

they then shouted and charged with bayonets across the open.

On the far flank of this British right wing Bose's Regiment became engaged with the riflemen of Campbell and lost men from the first moments. A confusing struggle in the heavy woods followed, with the Germans plunging after the riflemen, only to be shot from behind trees or felled with Indian axes. Harry Lee's men took part in this fight, which pressed on to the south and east for about a mile and lasted for two hours before Tarleton's horsemen were finally sent to rescue the Germans.

To the left of the road the action was much the same. Sergeant Lamb of the Fusileers was there with Webster:

"After the brigade formed across the open ground, the colonel rode on to the front and gave the word, 'Charge!' Instantly the movement was made, in excellent order, in a smart run, with arms charged. When arrived within forty yards of the enemy's line, it was perceived that their whole force had their arms presented and resting on a rail fence, the common partitions in America. They were taking aim with the nicest precision. . . . At this awful period a general pause took place; both parties surveyed each other for the moment with the most anxious suspense. . . . Colonel Webster rode forward in front of the 23rd Regiment and said with more than even his usual commanding voice (which was well known to his brigade), 'Come in, my brave Fuzileers!' This operated like an inspiring voice; they rushed forward amidst the enemy's fire; dreadful was the havoc on both sides."

The central segments of the American first line, those nearest the road on either side, had a strength of 1,060 men; with few exceptions these men broke for the rear during and after the first American volley, by some accident running for the flanks, so that the oncoming British would be exposed to the fire of the second line, in rear.

The men of Forbis did not flee, and several in the central line remained. One was Nathaniel Slade, a farmer from nearby Caswell County, who fired once and was reloading his rifle when he broke his ramrod. He borrowed a rod from his neighbor in the line and, when he looked up for a chance to fire, saw that the men around him had fled, and that the British were too near for him to get off a shot. He retreated; other men near him, he recalled, fired two rounds at the enemy.

The British cannon had ceased when the charge on the first line opened; they had fired for about twenty minutes and were now hitched behind their teams, moving in the great road as the infantry progressed. Lieutenant John McLeod herded them along. To his rear, out of musket range, was Tarleton's cavalry, held in reserve until needed to aid the infantry.

The American guns had now reached the rear, where they were placed on a flank of the third line.

The militia of the first line had largely disappeared, leaving the riflemen and cavalrymen on each flank fighting savagely against odds and withdrawing deeper into the woods.

The behavior of these North Carolinians was to be a matter of long controversy, but there was no doubt in Harry Lee's mind that they had performed badly:

> To our infinite distress and mortification, the North Carolina militia took to flight, a few only of Eaton's brigade excepted, who . . . manfully maintained their ground. Every effort was made by Generals Eaton and Butler, assisted by . . . many of the officers of every grade, to stop this un-

accountable panic, for not a man of the corps had been killed or even wounded. Lieutenant Colonel Lee joined in the attempt to rally the fugitives, threatening to fall upon them with his cavalry. All was vain—so thoroughly confounded were these unhappy men that, throwing away arms, knapsacks and even canteens, they rushed like a torrent headlong through the woods.

Greene thought that these militiamen had cost him victory on the spot:

> They had the most advantageous position I ever saw, and left it without making scarcely the shadow of opposition. Their general and field officers exerted themselves, but the men would not stand. Many threw away their arms and fled with the utmost precipitation, even before a gun was fired at them.

Until the militia had broken, the British right was in difficulty, where Campbell's riflemen and Lee's Legion were punishing the Bose Regiment. General Leslie had already called the Guards up from reserve, and fighting was becoming desperate. When the line collapsed before the British, however, Leslie turned the Bose and the Guards battalion against Lee, a move which cut the cavalrymen off from the army for the rest of the battle, Lee said.

Leslie then led the 71st Highlanders ahead, joining with Webster's left-hand force to launch an attack on the Virginians who waited in the second line.

The battle now roared in full fury and entered the growth of large timber, where the commanders could see little or nothing of its progress.

On the far right flank of the British, Lee and Campbell's riflemen moved slowly eastward. In the center, the Virginians of Lawson and Stevens, firing from behind trees and with their own sharpshooters in the rear to prevent flight, held firm. For about half an hour the second line held. The British files, broken by the trees, were further cut by the hidden riflemen, who often circled to snipe from the rear. On the British left the punishment was most severe, for William Washington, Kirkwood, and Lynch, when abandoned on the first line by the local militia, had fallen back to the flank of the Virginians and concentrated powerful fire against the Yagers, Light Infantry, and Thirty-third Regiments of the British. O'Hara was called up with the reserves on this side, the Grenadiers and Second Battalion of the Guards. These units finally pressed the Virginians from their position, forcing them to move stubbornly downhill toward the third line. Lynch's riflemen were driven off by the Thirty-third Regiment, which was freed for action by the coming of the reserves. First Lawson, and then Stevens, retreated. Stevens was wounded by a musket ball through a leg.

Except for the cavalry, every British unit had already come under heavy fire, and most of them had suffered significant casualties.

Greene thought the Virginia militia had "behaved nobly," but bravery was not universal. St. George Tucker witnessed a flight in this line, when some of his companions found the British coming up in their rear:

> Holcombe's regiment and ours instantly broke off without firing a single gun and dispersed like a flock of sheep frightened by dogs. . . . In attempting to rally a party of regular Troops I received a Wound in the small of my Leg from a soldier, who either from design or accident held his Bayonet in such a Direction that I could not possibly avoid it as I rode up to stop him from running away. . . .

Tucker and other officers collected some of these Virginians and fought in Indian fashion through the woods. They once passed a dying British officer against a tree, tended by an American rifleman who poured a drink of whiskey down his throat and urged him to die like a man. The militia rallied, joined the regulars in the rear, and fought until the action was over. Tucker was proud that they had stood to fire eighteen or twenty rounds at the enemy, after having been frightened from their position. He recalled wryly: "The Virginia militia had the honor to receive General Greene's thanks for their conduct. Some were undoubtedly entitled to them, while others ought to blush."

Until General Stevens was wounded and his discouraged men began to fall back, Banastre Tarleton, watching from the roadway, feared that the battle might be lost at the second line: "At this period the event of the action was doubtful, and victory alternately presided over each army."

The attacking British made little use of the bayonet in the underbrush, and their muskets could not match the American rifles under these conditions. The units were forced to break into small parties, some of which drove ahead rapidly and some of which were shattered; it was superior discipline which carried the second line of defense, after sheer numbers had failed.

The second line did not break until Cornwallis had left the road himself and gone on horseback to lead a charge. Sergeant Lamb saw him soon afterward:

I saw Lord Cornwallis riding across the clear ground. His Lordship was mounted on a dragoon's horse (his own having been shot); the saddle-bags were under the creature's belly, which much retarded his progress, owing to the vast quantity of underwood that was spread over the ground; His Lordship was evidently unconscious of his danger. I immediately laid hold of the bridle of his horse and turned his head. I then mentioned to him that if His Lordship had pursued the same direction, he would have been surrounded by the enemy and, perhaps, cut to pieces or captured. I continued to run along side of the horse, keeping the bridle in my hand, until His Lordship gained the 23rd Regiment, which was at that time drawn up in the skirt of the woods.

When the Virginians had disappeared before them, the Light Infantry of the Guards trotted down the wooded slope into the opening near the courthouse, where the final American line waited. The Yagers and the Thirty-third Regiment came up. Lieutenant Colonel Webster waited for little more than a casual glance at the veteran Continental troops in the line before him on the opposite slope. Webster ordered a charge.

The Guards struck the front of the First Maryland; Gunby's men drove them back with heavy casualties. The broken files were then pushed off the field by a counter-charge, and Webster's troops were led into the cover of woods on their left, where they formed in a ravine to wait for reinforcements. Webster had a gunshot wound in the knee which crippled him; within a few days he would die of it.

In the few moments of confusion which followed, American units swarmed out of the trees to join the third line. The men of Kirkwood and Lynch settled on the right of Huger's line. Other British units appeared, the First Battalion of the Guards in front, commanded by Lt. Col. Duncan Stuart. During this lull in the fighting Greene rode up and down the line of Continentals, urging the men to hold this position and drive off the enemy. The fight was almost an hour old. The final phase now opened.

Into the shallow valley of the small stream more British units trickled. Lieutenant Colonel Stuart led down the Second Battalion of the Guards and the Grenadiers. The young Scot had as little respect for the enemy line as Webster and, with one glance at the Continental line, led a charge.

Stuart saw only the Second Maryland Regiment, under Col. Benjamin Ford, since a patch of woods concealed Gunby and the First Maryland. Colonel Otho Williams rode behind Ford's line, shouting encouragement to them, expecting a repetition of the performance of Gunby's men. Williams was giving orders to combine the two Maryland regiments when to his surprise a panic broke out in the ranks of the Second Regiment and the line fell apart before the British attack. The two guns of Singleton, which were on the flank, were overrun and taken by the enemy.

The Second Maryland streamed away through the woods so swiftly that officers could not beat it back into position, though Greene himself made the attempt.

There was now hand-to-hand fighting in the narrow meadow. As Stuart's force charged after the running Second Maryland, Gunby attacked it in the flank, and William Washington came in with his cavalry, flying down the hillside unexpectedly. Stuart was killed by a sword wound from a captain of the First Maryland, the two cannon were retaken, and the Second Battalion and Grenadiers of the Guards were badly mauled. Washington's men chased many of them over the road and into the woods.

A spectacular soldier rode with Washington, one Peter Francisco, already the most famous private in the American army. He had been reared in Virginia, a castaway who had been discovered in expensive clothing on the seashore as an infant; he had become a blacksmith and, as a giant in young manhood, was reputedly the strongest man in Virginia. He had fought in the northern campaigns and had more than once refused a commission, saying that he lacked the learning to become an officer. He carried a huge sword and in the charge of Washington's dragoons was said to have killed eleven men in the fighting in the meadow, most of them members of the Guards. At the opening of the clash he had been pinned to his mount with a bayonet through his leg, had extricated himself with no sign of pain, then laid about him like a one-man cavalry troop.

Webster had rallied his men and was now in the meadow, but the pressure of the First Maryland's bayonets and Washington's troopers was forcing the entire mass backward from the meadow, toward Lord Cornwallis, who waited on the roadside. His Lordship ordered Lieutenant McLeod, the future Marquis of Lothian, to load his twin three-pounders with grapeshot and prepare to fire. McLeod begged him to wait, pointing out that he would be forced to fire into the backs of the Guards and would slaughter most of them. Cornwallis was adamant, even when the wounded General O'Hara came to beg that he hold his fire. The commander said that he must stop the American push or watch the army cut to pieces.

McLeod opened fire. Many of the Guards fell, and Cornwallis caused about half of his casualties in these bloody moments. The tide turned, however; Washington's charge was checked, and the troopers moved to the side. The Marylanders went back to their position, and the American guns were captured once more.

In the midst of this confused action William Washington rode within a few yards of a British officer who was surrounded by aides. The cavalryman guessed that it must be Cornwallis. He spurred his horse forward in an effort to capture him, but his helmet slipped over his face, blinding him for an instant, then falling from his head. As he dismounted to recover the helmet, the officer next to him, leading the cavalry column, was shot through the body and could not handle his horse. The animal wheeled and ran toward the rear; the dragoons followed him. Lee was left alone and robbed of his opportunity.

The hillside from which McLeod had fired, Colonel Tarleton judged, was the key to this terrain; if the Americans had seized it, the Royal artillery could not have swept the Continental line, and Cornwallis would have been driven from the field.

Furious fighting continued. Webster's men crossed the meadow and attacked the American right flank, where the Virginians and the Delaware regiment lay in line. The Welsh Fusileers and the 71st Highlanders, who had only now come into the open, joined the attack by moving on the First Maryland, now commanded by John Eager Howard in place of the wounded Gunby. There was another melee of bayonet fighting and firing at close range until word reached Greene that the Second Maryland could not be driven back into line, and that British infantrymen were reported moving in the rear of the Continentals.

The four cannon were already gone; there had been no horses to draw them off in the moment of danger and no time for men to pull them away. Greene was determined that he would not sacrifice his Continental infantry regiments as well. He issued orders to disengage.

Greene had often been in the midst of fighting, once so close to the action that he avoided capture only because of a screening hedge. He had not seen Harry Lee during the fighting and had not heard from him since the breaking of the first line. Lee's troopers had not been available when the brief

American offensive pushed the enemy across the bloody meadow. Mystery and controversy would swirl about Lee's role during the afternoon, but the cavalryman himself offered the story of his desperate fighting on the American left flank without apologies:

Borne off to the right by the Regiment of Bose and the Second Battalion of Guards, the Legion and the riflemen of Campbell fell back slowly, more than half a mile during the engagement, past the second line and finally to the rear of the third. Lee wrote of the final moments:

The long-impending contest upon the enemy's right continued without intermission, each of the combatants getting gradually nearer to the flanks of their respective armies, to close with which was the desired object of both.

When the British Guards left this field to join the main fighting, leaving Bose's Regiment to face the American flanking party, Lee at last detached his cavalry and led it to Greene. Lee arrived in the meadow too late to join the crucial attack, for Greene was pulling off his troops as the Legion riders appeared. Lee then turned to move his Legion infantry to the third line position but first had to extricate it from a skirmish of its own—an attempt to drive the Second Battalion of the Guards from a knoll formerly held by the Virginia militiamen. This minor action over, and the riflemen of Campbell still fending off the Germans of the Bose Regiment, Lee joined Greene.

The Virginia horseman had been out of major action from the start, behaving as if he were in independent command. Critics were to say that he should have communicated with Greene and explained his situation rather than withholding his cavalry at will. His skirmishing had not been desperate since the first moments of the battle, and he might have spared part of his force at any time. Greene, on the other hand, seems not to have sent for Lee.

Harry Lee assumed that Greene had dismissed the Legion from his mind, once the flank force had been pushed aside by the first British offensive, and thus had no longer thought of the Virginia shock troops as available to him. Lee thought the Quaker had retreated too soon: "Had General Greene known how severely his enemy was crippled, and that the corps under Lee had fought their way to his Continental line, he would certainly have continued the conflict."

As it was, the Americans pulled back skillfully, leaving a stubborn rear guard of Virginians under Col. John Greene, who was grumbling because he had seen little action for the day. The Virginia and Delaware regulars under Huger were still fighting with Webster's force when it broke off by files and moved rearward. Otho Williams brought off the Marylanders and others who had settled behind them. There was no effort to save the guns. There was scattered firing along the route of retreat.

Lee's cavalry went eastward along the great road, without pursuit until it found a crossroad to the north and got into the track of the main army. The 71st Highlanders and the Welsh Fusileers followed the infantry for a mile or so but were soon called off. Greene halted three miles from the field to collect stragglers and fugitives and then moved on to his old camp at the ironworks on Troublesome Creek. He had fought for just over two hours.

The last action on the field was by Tarleton, who was sent to the far right to drive off Campbell's riflemen, who had so roughly handled the Bose Regiment. Tarleton found the

mountaineers already moving off, but his leading sections
were stung by rifle fire from behind trees, and he did not
push the enemy.

Tarleton was otherwise inactive during the day, and
though he recalled that "Earl Cornwallis did not think it ad-
visable for the British cavalry to charge the enemy," St. George
Tucker of the Virginians had another recollection:

> Our Militia joined the Virginia Regulars under Colonel
> Campbell, and sustained a good smart fire for some minutes.
> We were soon ordered to retreat. Whilst we were doing so
> Tarleton advanced to attack us with his horse, but a party
> of continentals who were fortunately close behind us gave
> him so warm a reception that he retreated with some degree
> of precipitation. A few minutes after we halted by the side
> of an old field fence and observed him with his Legion
> surveying us at the distance of two or three hundred yards.
> He did not think proper to attack us again as we were ad-
> vantageously posted and the continentals who had en-
> countered him just before were still in our rear.

There was a more serious disagreement over these last
moments of the battle on the flank. The last stand of Campbell's riflemen had been atop a long slope, from which the
Guards and the Bose Regiment drove them after painful and
costly work. Once the British won the hilltop, however, riflemen appeared in their rear and began picking off the infantry
in their bright coats. It was in response to this fire that Cornwallis had sent Tarleton. While the German regiment fired a
volley, Tarleton had charged in an effort to rout the last of
the Americans.

Colonel Campbell reported indignantly that Lee's Legion
was within 200 yards of the action when this was taking
place, but rode past as if he saw nothing. Lee denied the accu-

sation with some heat, but Campbell was not swayed and within a few days resigned from the army in protest.

It had been a cold, clear, sunny day, with little wind, and as the fighting ended there was increased suffering among the wounded lying in the shaded woods. Shortly before nightfall a storm rolled in from the northwest, and there was a driving rain which lasted through the night. Harry Lee described the plight of Cornwallis, who had won the ground:

Nearly a third of his force slaughtered, many of his best officers killed or wounded, and that victory for which he had so long toiled, and at last gained, bringing in its trail not one solitary benefit. No body of loyalists crowding around his standards, no friendly convoys pouring in supplies, his wants pressing and his resources distant. The night succeeding this day of blood was rainy, dark and cold; the dead unburied, the wounded unsheltered, the groans of the dying and the shrieks of the living cast a deeper gloom.

Stedman, the historian, who went over the field in his work as quartermaster, found dead and wounded scattered over a large area of the field. He estimated that at least fifty men died during the night.

Greene took his army through the storm without pause, but it was almost daylight of Mar. 16 when he reached the old camp at the ironworks. Troops at once went to work improving the defenses of the place by throwing up earthworks. Morale was strangely high, and throughout the camp there was talk of another battle. Stragglers and new parties of militia came in through the day. The camp was about ten miles to the northeast of the battlefield, and dispatch riders moved between the armies. Greene's first act was to send back a surgeon to treat the American wounded. His soldiers grinned over a camp tale during the day: Cornwallis had sent in an officer under a flag of truce, pointing out that Greene had been driven off with the loss of all his cannon, and that he should now surrender. The Quaker was reported to have replied: "I am ready to sell His Lordship another field at the same price."

Greene's orders of the day were both belligerent and prudent: "The General requests the officers will take every precaution to procure their arms and ammunition, and make every necessary preparation for another field day."

But the General's health, never robust, was near the breaking point. He had not taken off his clothes for six weeks of constant campaigning and had seldom spent a night in a bed. He fainted on the first night in the camp at Troublesome and collapsed again the following night. He wrote to his wife, concealing his condition, saying, "our fatigue has been excessive . . . but am generally in pretty good health." He was not in despair:

> . . . The action was long, bloody and severe. . . . I had not the honor of being wounded, but I was very near being taken, having rode in the heat of the action full tilt into the midst of the enemy. . . .
>
> Our army, though obliged to give up the ground, retired in good order, and the enemy suffered so severely that they dare not move towards us. . . . Nothing but blood and slaughter prevail here, and the operations are in a country little short of a wilderness. . . . How uncertain are human affairs. I should be extremely happy if the war had an honorable close, and I on a farm with my little family about me.

Greene was even more optimistic in his report to Joseph Reed in Congress, saying that except for winning the ground and the artillery, the British had no advantage:

On the contrary, they are little short of being ruined. The enemy's loss in killed and wounded cannot be less than between six and seven hundred, perhaps more. . . .

Never did an army labor under so many disadvantages as this; but the fortitude and patience of the officers and soldiery rise superior to all difficulties. We have little to eat, less to drink, and lodge in the woods in the midst of smoke. . . .

Our army is in good spirits, but the militia are leaving us in great number to return home to kiss their wives and sweethearts.

At the close of his report Green revealed the most significant result of the long retreat and the savage battle:

I have never felt an easy moment since the enemy crossed the Catawba, until the defeat of the 15th. But now I am perfectly easy, persuaded it is out of the enemy's power to do us any great injury. Indeed, I think they will retire as soon as they can get off their wounded.

The Quaker, for all his bitterness toward the militiamen who had cost him victory, realized that he had won a campaign; for the first time, he was confident that the south could not be conquered by the invaders. He wrote George Washington to complain that he could never acquire a military reputation through defeat, while operating under such handicaps, but he seemed to be wrestling with a personal vanity. It was clear to him that the war had taken a new turn; the savagery with which most of his men had resisted the British veterans at Guilford was like nothing he had seen during the Revolution.

No one could tot up the casualties with accuracy. The official report of Greene's losses listed a total of 1,255 men, but most of these were "missing," and officers knew that the militia had merely gone to their homes.

Of the missing men, the reports of Otho Williams showed that Stevens's regiment had 121, Lawson's 87, and the riflemen of both Campbell and Lynch, 94. This was a total of 302 missing Virginians.

The regiments of Butler and Eaton had 561 missing, and one other North Carolina band, that of Capt. Arthur Forbis, made no report. Forbis was dead.

Williams said that most of the missing were assumed to have gone home, and that there was evidence in their guns, which they had thrown down on the field. (The British soon reported the discovery and destruction of 1,300 muskets and rifles on the field, evidently discarded by the militia.)

Greene had suffered relatively little in dead and wounded. The Virginians had 11 dead and 67 wounded, and the North Carolinians reporting had 7 dead and 6 wounded.

The serious losses were in the small force of the Continentals, the backbone of the southern army. Officially, there were 290 casualties among the regulars (though Harry Lee put the loss at 14 officers and 312 rank and file—very few of these missing).

A British report challenged these facts, saying that the houses for miles around were filled with American wounded for some days after the battle.

The serious losses in officers were limited: Generals Isaac Huger and Edward Stevens and Col. John Gunby were wounded, and Major Anderson of the Maryland troops was dead.

The Quaker did not take seriously his militia losses; he realized that they would be made up by recruits if he were successful, and he was aware of their faults to the point of violent prejudice: "It is astonishing to me how these people could place such a confidence in a militia scattered over the face of the whole earth. . . . The militia in the back country are formidable, the others are not, and all are very ungovernable and difficult to keep together. As they have generally come out, twenty thousand might be in motion, and not five hundred in the field."

Greene berated the militia in every letter from his headquarters, and his reports persuaded the North Carolina legislature to sentence militiamen of the counties around Guilford to serve eighteen months in the army as punishment for their behavior at Guilford Courthouse. Later critics attributed some of Greene's ire to the fact that he was working for a large force of American regulars, as a standing army in war or peace.

This view did not blind the Quaker to the value of the men at hand, and when, on Mar. 17, a band of mounted North Carolina infantry reported under the French adventurer Colonel Malmedy, he sent it to roam the counties south of Hillsboro, where Tories were said to be ravaging the countryside.

Joseph Reed, the President of Congress, warned Greene that he must not go too far in condemnation of the militia, since a show of superiority by Continental officers would alienate "the bulk of the country."

Charles Cornwallis had been wounded in the hand but refused to allow himself to be listed among the casualties. Neighbors reported that he made headquarters for the night in the little cabin of Joseph Hoskins, and that the loft was filled with his wounded. Lights gleamed on the field through the night, as British parties collected the wounded, both their own and American. The day after the battle people of the region watched redcoats dig long trenches in the yard of the Hoskins house, where they piled a large number of bodies.

Cornwallis had usually overestimated the strength of his enemy during the campaign and did not err on the liberal side when reporting his own. His casualty rolls revealed a staggering toll:

Of his total strength of about 2,400, about 1,950 had been on the site of the battle (Lieutenant Colonel Hamilton had one regiment, supported by a hundred more infantry and twenty dragoons, guarding the baggage in the rear).

The losses were 93 dead, 413 wounded, and 26 missing. This amounted to more than a fourth of the British on the field, including a number of important officers. Lieutenant Colonel Duncan Stuart of the Guards and Lieutenant O'Hara of the artillery, a brother of the General, were dead. Brigadier Generals O'Hara and Howard and Lieutenant Colonels Tarleton and Webster were wounded, the latter fatally. Nine captains were wounded, two of them in the Bose Regiment.

These were not a mystery to Cornwallis, who was said to have reflected on the battle: "Such fighting I have not seen since God made me. The Americans fought like demons."

Harry Lee had an explanation for the greater losses of the British:

> We had great advantage in the ground, and were sheltered . . . until the enemy approached very near, while he was exposed from first to last. We had spent the previous day in ease . . . he had been preparing during the day, and marching part of the night. We were acquainted with wood and tree fighting; he ignorant of both. And lastly, we

were trained to take aim and fire low, he was not so trained, and from this cause, or from the composition of his cartridge (too much powder for the lead) he always overshot.

Cornwallis did not report the incident in which he inflicted so many of his own casualties, beyond saying that the artillery was used. Colonel Tarleton spoke only of "the judicious use of the three-pounders"—but the army did not forget the price paid for victory or his Lordship's firm insistence on the firing of grapeshot through the Guards.

One of the most courageous and dependable of his Lordship's fighting units during the battle had been the Bose Regiment, under Col. Christian DuPuy (or DuBuy), which had stubbornly followed Lee's Legion and Campbell's riflemen. All of this struggle had been beyond the view of Cornwallis, but the casualty returns indicated the nature of the work. Some later critics gave credit to the Germans for carrying the field for the Earl.

Captain Wilmousky of this regiment was killed, as was a lieutenant, Ernst von Trott. Among the wounded were Capt. Johann Eigenbrod and Lt. Johann Josias Geyso.

The Germans who had fought at Guilford were the survivors of the war's most severe campaigning, and the men in ranks were those who had suffered from long marches with poor food and little shelter; some of their companions had deserted in the backcountry. In newspapers in London and occupied New York there was much praise for the conduct of the regiment at Guilford, and one of the German rulers who had hired the troops to England, the Elector Friedrick, wrote: "I have heard, with great pleasure, of the good conduct of the von Bose Regiment, under Lt. Col. DuPuy, and of the Yagers, under Capt. Ewald, and request you to make known to these officers and their command my satisfaction."

There was little the British could do for the wounded who survived the night after the battle. The army had marched many miles before going into action and had no baggage; it would take time for wagons to come up. There were no tents, and the cabins and barns of the neighborhood were too few to accommodate all. The redcoats had not eaten all day, and the day before had had short rations in midafternoon, a quarter-pound of flour and a quarter-pound of stringy beef for each man. Two days after the battle, Cornwallis reported that he had to send more than nine miles in every direction to find forage in the depleted country. When the only mill in the neighborhood broke down from overuse, orders of the day announced that his Lordship was "thoroughly sensible of the distress" suffered by the troops for lack of meal and flour. He urged the men to be patient, reminding them that they were obliged to stay in this camp until the wounded had been cared for. It was obvious that at least seventy must be left behind.

On Mar. 17 he sent seventeen wagons loaded with wounded toward the New Garden Friends Meeting, to the west, under heavy guard and with an insistent order: "Each wagon to carry as many of the wounded men as can possibly be put into it." A later order of the day revealed the beginning of a retreat:

All the women of the army except one a company, to be immediately sent after the wounded men of the army.

Cornwallis did everything possible to embellish the victory. His orders to the army praised its "extraordinary valor," and added that he considered it "the greatest honor of my life to have been placed at the head of so gallant an army." He called the names of many officers.

On Mar. 18, when he had moved to New Garden, Corn-

wallis made use of the Royal governor, Martin, and the print-
ing press he carried with him. There was another proclamation designed to bolster the Tories:

> Whereas, by the blessing of Almighty God, His Maj-
> esty's arms have been crowned with signal success, by the
> complete victory obtained over the rebel forces on the 15th
> instant, I . . . call upon all loyal subjects to stand forth and
> take an active part in restoring good order and govern-
> ment. . . .

He went so far as to offer pardons to all rebels, except
murderers, who would surrender themselves within a month.
Stedman recorded that the lord was "greatly disappointed in
his expectation of being joined by the loyalists. Some of them
indeed came within the lines, but they remained only a few
days."

The wagons and supplies had come up from Bell's Mills
late on the day after the battle, but these stores were quickly
depleted. Little or nothing had been gleaned from the battlefield beyond American arms. These included the four brass
six-pounders, 160 round shot, fifty case shot, and two ammunition wagons. The 1,300 captured muskets and rifles were
broken or burned, except for those passed out to Tories in
the region.

On Sunday, Mar. 18, when they had finished their burials
—one report said they burned some of the bodies—the British
moved to New Garden, where they spent the night. The only
depredation near the courthouse was the burning of the house
of one Campbell, reputedly a Whig. On Mar. 19, the invaders moved down the Deep River to Bell's Mills, where
they stopped for two days.

Cornwallis now intended to move southeastward through
the State to Wilmington, where he could get supplies and

reinforcements by sea. On the way, he would stop at Cross Creek, on the upper Cape Fear, to replenish his stores. His report to Clinton on the battle gave brief explanation as to why he did not chase Greene:

> The great fatigue of the troops, the number of wounded, the want of provisions, preventing our pursuing the enemy beyond Reedy Fork. . . . If the reinforcements from Europe have arrived, send the whole or the greatest part to Wilmington, with orders to proceed without loss of time to Cross Creek.

Word of the battle swept through the country. In Charleston the occupying forces ordered every house illuminated, and the troops fired salutes; there was a victory ball. New York Tories and the British army staged less spectacular celebrations, though there was a report that Cornwallis had taken 1,600 prisoners and crushed the rebellion in the south. The British garrison at Fort George in the far north built a bonfire in celebration.

In London, the dour Charles Fox told Parliament: "Another such victory would be the ruin of the British army." The *London Magazine* hailed Guilford as a glorious victory which would bring the Carolinas and Virginia back into the Royal fold. But the *Annual Register*, of Whig leanings, said: "That victory . . . was productive of all the consequences of defeat." Horace Walpole said tersely: "Lord Cornwallis has conquered his troops out of shoes and provision, and himself out of troops." He predicted that the battle boded ultimate defeat for the British in America.

Nathanael Greene recovered quickly, and on Mar. 18, as if he needed only word that he was no longer the hare but the hound, he turned the army after Cornwallis. The British had a lead of forty miles.

Henry Lee had first urged action, regardless of the worn condition of the commander and his army. Greene was forced to wait for a day or two for lack of ammunition but sent his light troops southward as boldly as ever. If he had tender feelings about Lee's work at Guilford Courthouse, he gave no sign:

Nine o'clock P.M. March 18, 1781

Lieutenant-Colonel Lee:—

I have this moment got your note. I am perfectly agreed with you in opinion, that to attack the enemy on their march will be best. I have written to Colonel Williams for that purpose.

It will be next to impossible to get the militia to send away their horses. They are so attached to this method of carrying on the war, that they will not listen to any other. . . . However, we can try the experiment. Sound some of the more sensible on the subject. My letter must be short, as I write in pain.

N. GREENE

Lee took with him some infantry under Campbell, mostly riflemen, and struck almost due south between the Deep and the Haw, a more direct route to the Cape Fear River than Cornwallis had followed. Before the British left Bell's Mills, on the morning of Mar. 21, the American guerrilla parties were hacking at their outposts. There were frequent skirmishes. Still Cornwallis moved slowly, as if aware that Greene had not approached with his main body. The armies drifted down the masked watercourse to the mill of Thomas Dixon on Cane Creek, a few miles from Bell's, where the British buried some dead in a Quaker churchyard, dug a well, and slaughtered eighty cattle and several sheep. Neighbors reported to the Americans that two cannon had been dropped into the well—and that many British officers were being carried in two-horse litters.

Greene was now coming near with the infantry, and the British moved downstream to Ramsey's Mill, the lowest mill on the river. Tarleton reported action on the way: "The day before the King's troops arrived at Ramsey's the Americans insulted the Yagers in their encampment." That was not the only incident, for each time British soldiers took horses to drink in the shallows near the mill, riflemen fired from ambush, and troopers had to flounder through the thickets to drive off the tormentors.

The British spent two days at Ramsey's, taking in provisions and building a crude bridge, and when word of this reached Greene, the chase became more rapid. Except for a breach of discipline the Quaker could have caught the enemy at this crossing.

When he was two days out of the Troublesome Creek camp, he held an inspection of arms and ammunition and found that some of the men, all militia, had traded powder and lead for food and drink. Greene lost another day in bringing up more ammunition.

It was a near thing, even so. The American vanguard came so unexpectedly to the riverside that the British left some of their dead unburied, and the rear guard was able to do no more than partially destroy the bridge they had made. Greene's men were so hungry that they turned aside in the British camp, fighting for scraps from the piles of offal where cattle had been slaughtered, swallowing grisly scraps not yet claimed by the vultures.

Greene paused briefly to allow some of his militia to go

home, their enlistments having expired; the British dropped burdens, too, including prisoners taken on the route. Greene no longer pressed the chase, but his determination was made clear in an order to Lee:

> I mean to fight the enemy again, and wish you to have your Legion and riflemen ready for action on the shortest notice. If in the mean time you can attempt anything which promises an advantage, put it in execution. Lord Cornwallis must be soundly beaten before he relinquishes his hold.

Scouts following Cornwallis found him well on the road to Cross Creek, through a country of sand barrens which had been pillaged by Tories and Whigs in a bloody civil war now ten years old. Greene saw that he could not prevent the British from camping in the river town on the navigable Cape Fear, where they could draw supplies from Wilmington.

Near the end of March, Cornwallis crossed to the east bank of the Cape Fear and moved for Wilmington itself, leaving open the way into South Carolina, where the long chase had begun. The chain of British forts in the interior of that State made a tempting target. Greene moved to strike it and to clear the enemy from the far south.

Epilogue

CHARLES CORNWALLIS MOVED INTO THE LARGEST HOUSE IN the little town of Wilmington, twelve miles up the Cape Fear from the sea, and gave his army a rest. Life was pleasant in the port town, with a horde of slaves to tend the General and his staff in the comfortable white mansion.

The Earl was too astute to accept the rhetoric of his proclamations. He knew that a campaign had ended, and that his invading force was by no means a conquering band.

His companion in arms, Maj. Gen. William Phillips, had lately invaded Virginia from the sea and was planning a campaign in that province. Three days after he had arrived in Wilmington, Cornwallis wrote him in complete candor:

> I have had a most difficult and dangerous campaign, and was obliged to fight a battle 200 miles from any communication, against an enemy seven times my number. The fate of it was long doubtful. We had not a regiment or a corps that did not at sometime give way; it ended however happily by completely routing the enemy and taking their cannon.

The idea of our friends rising in any number and to any purpose totally failed, as I expected, and here I am getting rid of my wounded and refitting my troops at Wilmington.

I heard last night of the naval action and your arrival in the Chesapeake. Now, my dear friend, what is our plan? Without one we cannot succeed, and I assure you that I am quite tired of marching about the country in quest of adventure. If we mean an offensive war in America we must abandon New York and bring our whole force into Virginia; we then have a state to fight for, and a successful battle may give us America. If our plan is defensive, mixed with desultory expeditions, let us quit the Carolinas (which cannot be held defensively while Virginia can be so easily armed against us) and stick to our salt pork at New York, sending now and then detachments to steal tobacco, etc.

I daily expect three regiments from Ireland; leaving one of them at Charleston and with the addition of the other two and the flank companies I can come by land to you; but whether after we have joined we shall have sufficient force for a war of conquest, I should think very doubtful.

By war of conquest I mean, to possess the country sufficiently to overturn the rebel government, and to establish a militia and some kind of mixed authority of our own. If no reinforcements come, and I am obliged to march with my present force to the upper frontiers of South Carolina, my situation will be truly distressing. If I was to embark from hence, the loss of the upper posts in South Carolina would be inevitable. . . .

He added that he had no orders from Sir Henry Clinton in New York—and that he could not be sure even of getting this letter through to Phillips, because of "the vigilance and severity" of the rebel government. He also warned that he must soon leave the North Carolina port to avoid sickness among his men and horses.

A few days later his returns showed that, of his fewer than 2,200 men, there were 397 wounded and 436 sick—casting suspicion upon the official casualty rolls after Guilford.

This prophetic letter was one of the most remarkable documents the war was to produce. It accurately forecast the defeat of the British in Virginia—at Yorktown—and equally as accurately exposed the cause of that defeat. The indecision brought on by the distance and clash of opinion between Cornwallis and his chief, Clinton, had resulted in heavy losses as the column beat through the backcountry after Greene. Having failed to destroy the Quaker's army, Cornwallis was left without the fruits of victory.

The remedy for the situation, if there was one, was set forth by Cornwallis months in advance of the end. The able officer whose reputation was to survive surrender at Yorktown and increase when he became Commander in Chief in India was almost alone, among officers of both armies, in glimpsing the military shape of things to come. Long after the revolution was over the voluminous correspondence of controversy between Cornwallis and Clinton was to rake over every detail of the war in the south, in an attempt to fix blame for the loss of America. The key to it all might have been found in this Cornwallis letter of Apr. 10, 1781.

The Earl wrote to Clinton on the same day, and though his meaning was plain, his appeal was more subtle—too subtle, it developed:

> Until Virginia is in a manner subdued, our hold of the Carolinas must be difficult, if not precarious. The Rivers in Virginia are advantageous to an invading army; but North Carolina is of all the provinces in America the most difficult to attack. . . .

He did not say it in as many words, but Cornwallis realized fully that the toll of guerrilla fighting from Cowpens to Guilford Courthouse and the heavy casualties of the two pitched battles of the campaign threatened the collapse of British power in America. He must leave North Carolina or be pinned against the sea at Wilmington; if he went into South Carolina to defend his outposts, he was doomed; if he went north into Virginia, the most logical target, South Carolina would collapse. In short, the only solution was to persuade Clinton to give up the comfortable post he had held so long in New York and come south into the field for a final, decisive action. It was not to be.

Clinton had sent reinforcements to Phillips in Virginia, and with a cooperating force under Benedict Arnold they were to skirmish in leisurely fashion with the little army of Lafayette during the summer months ahead.

Cornwallis had done no more than warn the commander in South Carolina, the youthful general, Lord Francis Rawdon, who was at Camden: Cornwallis was 150 miles distant with several large rivers between the two forces, so that if Greene moved south, he could not follow him effectively.

When he learned that Greene had indeed marched for South Carolina, Cornwallis wrote to Clinton, Phillips, and other officers, almost as if in indignation at a personal affront. He told Phillips:

> Greene took advantage of my being obliged to come to this place, and has marched to South Carolina. My expresses to Lord Rawdon . . . warning him of the possibility of such a movement, have all failed—I much fear that Lord Rawdon's posts will be so distant from each other, and his troops so scattered, as to put him into the greatest danger of being beat in detail.

It was an exact picture of what was to come in South Carolina. But the enemy found Cornwallis less certain in his daily moves than he was in correspondence. Harry Lee's scouts reported that the British vanguard once went so far as to cross to the southern bank of the Cape Fear, as if to march to the rescue of Rawdon; it was soon recalled. Lee made his estimate of the British plight:

> If, as I believe, a general is sure to act wisely when he takes the course most dreaded by his adversary, the decision of General Greene was indubitably correct. For never was a leader more affected than Cornwallis was, by the disclosure of his enemy's object. Day after day did His Lordship revolve in his mind the difficulties of his situation, seeking the most eligible course . . .
>
> Sometimes he determined to follow Greene into South Carolina, and to punish him for his temerity; at other times he would proceed to Virginia, and by the rapidity of his success in that quarter, compel Greene to abandon his object, and hasten to its relief. At length he decided in favor of the latter measure, persuaded that Greene had gained so much time as would probably enable him to strike his first blow. . . . The reasoning was plausible, but not solid.

Thus the armies which had skirmished for so long through the Carolinas separated, and Cornwallis moved up the North Carolina coast and into the Virginia tidewater country. His commander, Henry Clinton, was displeased:

> In the disordered state of Carolina and Georgia, as represented to me . . . I shall dread what may be the consequence of Your Lordship's move unless a reinforcement arrives very soon in South Carolina. Had it been possible for Your Lordship in your letter to me of the 10th to have intimated the probability of your intention to form a junction with General Phillips, I should certainly have en-

deavored to have stopped you—as I did then, as well as now, consider such a move as likely to be dangerous to our interest in the Southern colonies.

The British cause thus drifted toward the disaster of Yorktown, despite the awareness of the high command that all was not right with its strategic plans. Josiah Martin, the deposed governor of North Carolina, realizing that he was the last of the Royal line, gave up the fight and sailed for England; he gave ill health as the cause.

An early American critic of Cornwallis and his campaign was the President of Congress, Joseph Reed:

Like a desolating meteor, he has passed, carrying destruction and distress to individuals—his army has walked through the country, daily adding to the number of its enemies, and leaving their few friends exposed to every punishment for their ill-timed and ill-placed confidence.

Greene's own estimate of the terrible days of the winter was almost humble:

Here has been the field for the exercise of genius, and an opportunity to practice all the great and little arts of war. Fortunately we have blundered through without meeting with capital misfortune.

Some admiring officers in the British service were more complimentary. Frederick Mackenzie, who was serving in the north, wrote:

Greene is entitled to great praise for his wonderful exertions; the more he is beaten the farther he advances in the end. He has been indefatigable in collecting troops and leading them to be defeated.

Other observant Britons had seen that the talents of Greene and other American leaders would be most dangerous in the small actions which took place almost daily, most of them never to be recorded. As early as 1775 General Hervey had written General Howe: "Our army will be destroyed by damned driblets . . . America is an ugly job . . . a damned affair indeed." Six years later, when Greene had completed his withdrawal against Cornwallis, the *Annual Register* said solemnly from London:

> Most of these actions would in other wars be considered as skirmishes of little account, and scarcely worthy of a detailed narrative. But these small actions are as capable as any of displaying military conduct. The operations of war being spread over that vast continent, by the new plan that was adopted, it is by such skirmishes that the fate of America must be necessarily decided. They are therefore as important as battles in which a hundred thousand are drawn up on each side.

Cornwallis had not only been forced to realize this unpalatable truth—that the exasperating skirmishes of his route had been all-important. He had by now accepted the more difficult conception that victory was by no means always what it seemed. Morgan had butchered Tarleton at Cowpens and been forced to flee; he had overpowered Greene at Guilford Courthouse and could do nothing but fall back. Short of the destruction of armies and the absolute subjugation of the people, there was no victory. They had taught no such warfare in the academy at Turin.

To Nathanael Greene, the prospect was by no means glorious, once Cornwallis had gone to Wilmington. He wrote to George Washington at the end of March, despairing of raising enough troops anywhere in the south—for neither Maryland nor North Carolina had sent a single man in response to his recent calls. If the British went to the sea, he said, "They will be in a position where it would be impossible for us to injure them if we had a force." Greene then an-nounced—he did not propose—the move which broke British resistance in the south and made Yorktown virtually inevitable. He wrote this from the remote backwoods post at Ramsey's Mill on the Haw River, where his soldiers were feasting on the offal piles of British cattle pens, at a time when the bulk of his militia was preparing to leave for home:

> In this critical and distressing situation, I am determined to carry the war immediately into South Carolina. The enemy will be obliged to follow us, or give up their posts in that state. If the former takes place, it will draw the war out of this state, and give it an opportunity to raise its proportion of men. If they leave their posts to fall, they must lose more than they can gain here. If we continue in this state, the enemy will hold their possession in both. All things considered, I think the movement is warranted by the soundest reasons, both political and military. . . .
>
> I am persuaded the movement will be unexpected to the enemy, and I intend it shall be as little known as possible. . . . I shall take every measure to avoid a misfortune, but necessity obliges me to commit myself to change; and I trust my friends will do justice to my reputation if any accident befalls me.

He wrote Governor Nash of North Carolina the same day, calling for twenty hogsheads of rum for the troops: "Without spirits the men cannot support the fatigues of the campaign." He wrote Marion, Sumter, and Pickens with orders to stir up the backcountry and be ready to join the offensive.

In early April, when he got word of the march, Harry Lee wrote his chief:

> I am decidedly of opinion with you, that nothing is left for you but to imitate the example of Scipio Africanus.

This may eventually undo the successes gained by the enemy the last campaign, and must probably render abortive every effort of His Lordship to establish himself in this state.

I am conscious that no general, in any period, undertook an enterprise more glorious. I am also conscious that no general ever commanded troops worse appointed or worse supplied than those which form your present army.

On Apr. 6 the Quaker turned south, to the campaign which was to bring him to severe engagements at Hobkirk's Hill, Ninety Six, and Eutaw Springs and drive the British occupation force to the sea. Greene felt almost as if no one else in the country knew that he was marching, or that the nation's life was at stake: "All the way through the country as I passed I found the people engaged in matters of interest, and in pursuit of pleasure, almost regardless of their danger . . . every man excusing himself from giving the least aid to the Government, from the apprehension that they would get no return for any advances."

Behind him in Virginia, affairs were confused. Greene had ordered von Steuben to send him reinforcements, but when Phillips and Arnold had landed in Virginia, the Council and Governor Jefferson had refused to allow their troops to leave, whatever the situation in the south. Steuben fell into a squabble with Virginia officials and no help was sent. Greene wrote young Lafayette of his anger at Jefferson, saying that it was "extremely wrong for a Governor of a State to undertake from partial views to counteract a general plan." The Virginians were also still squabbling over the seizure of their horses by the army during the winter and now demanded payment. The Quaker was finally stung to write Jefferson: "Are your horses dearer than your liberty?"

The Lessons

L ONG BEFORE THE FIRST OF THE SQUIRREL RIFLES FLAMED on the field at Cowpens, the young campaign had broken with classic military tradition. The Indian wars had prepared both Britons and Americans for the shock of backwoods fighting—but by now British veterans of the frontier were few, and most Americans were little better prepared.

As Nathanael Greene said, it was the backwoodsmen, the mountaineers who waged an almost daily fight for life, who made the difference:

> The back country people are bold and daring, but the people upon the seashore are sickly, and but indifferent militia.

Except for the superb cavalry on its Virginia plantation horses, the fine American militia troops came from the mountain regions. Those who ran from battle were generally from the piedmont and coastal areas, men whose lives had been relatively soft and easy for a generation, who had never known the Indian menace, and who no longer depended on the forests for food.

It was this kind of strength which was epitomized in Daniel Morgan—literally a different race from the British regulars or the American lowcountrymen. The frontiersmen, illiterate by and large, in civilian life objects of contempt to their eastern superiors, gave Nathanael Greene and Daniel Morgan the key to victory in the winter of 1781.

The men of the southern mountains had given the Americans their first victory in the south in October, two months before Greene arrived to take over his pitifully small command in Charlotte. Kings Mountain still haunted the British camp and hampered the movements of Charles Cornwallis. It was this victory, and the quality of his backwoods manpower, that enabled Greene to violate the first principle of warfare in his first strategic decision. If he had not divided his inferior force in front of the enemy, the course of the war might well have changed.

Once Greene had sent Morgan to the west and moved to Cheraw to rest the main army, he had no reason to expect victory from the Old Wagoner. Neither Briton nor American conceived of another Kings Mountain until the very moment when the tide turned at Cowpens.

Morgan's officers, men of experience, were dismayed by the choice of the American defensive position. Tarleton's own inspection of the lines convinced him that he could have asked no more favorable field—and he never changed that opinion. There was valor enough in both armies and opportunity for either infantry to break for the rear; Morgan had guarded against this by placing riflemen in the rear to halt a panic, the result of frontier lessons.

It was not until John Howard found the time ripe to charge with the bayonet, flinging the First Maryland into an unfamiliar role, and William Washington came on at a charge, that the issue was decided. Even Morgan had misunderstood Howard's preliminary move.

The Continental troops and Washington's cavalry were the final instruments of this victory, but the frontier riflemen gave them the opportunity. The British files were broken and virtually officerless after the opening rifle volleys, and this cost the redcoats discipline in the crucial moments. This was not a series of accidents, but the natural outgrowth of Morgan's knowledge of his men and their weapons, and of the nature of the enemy. He was, after the battle of Camden the previous summer, one of the few regular officers in the south who saw through the myth of the invincibility of British veterans. His riflemen at Saratoga had won the most important victory in the north.

Cowpens was instructive to Greene, who followed its pattern consciously when he had come to earth at Guilford Courthouse; it was apparently a lesson lost upon Cornwallis. Tarleton never fathomed it, and in his mind it remained a mystery—except for the teaching that an extended line of infantry, strung out at length, was at a disadvantage against three successive lines of waiting men, even when backed by artillery.

The days after Cowpens were equally important: Morgan was almost overcome with joy at the unexpected victory, which was almost complete. Yet within moments after the guns ceased, he was planning his flight. Lesser generals, more vain of their military reputation and without a long experience in irregular frontier fighting, might have waited on the battlefield. Morgan's flight was instinctive, and its marches were conducted with great skill, though in such unassuming fashion that historians were to overlook the effects of his dancing around Cornwallis. Though rheumatism (or more likely a ruptured disk of the spinal column) felled him when he reached the Catawba, he attended to every essential detail of retreat and prepared to defend himself at the river.

The reaction of Cornwallis was marred by anger, which evidently distracted him from making a study of the battle and the cause of defeat. His moves in the first few days of pursuit were the most damaging of his campaign, and he seemed in those days less the able soldier than before or after.

Cowpens literally destroyed the light corps of the British army in the south: The infantry of Tarleton's Legion, a battalion from the Seventh and Seventy-first Regiments of infantry, and many of the 17th Light Dragoons all went into American prison pens, or were buried in the wilderness cattleyard. The loss was about nine hundred men, all of them long-trained, exposed to battle, and hard marching—troops of a sort which might have made a difference in the Virginia fighting before Yorktown and would surely have increased the burdens of Nathanael Greene in the two months of the Carolina campaign. Cowpens cost Cornwallis at least a third of his power, and more in mobility.

Cowpens had an enduring appeal for military men and historians, most of whom dwelt upon the intricacies of the movements, some of them unexpected, growing from the use of Morgan's triple lines. The cardinal lesson to both armies at the moment, however, was that American troops, intelligently led and their limitations recognized, could be persuaded to stand against the British soldiers and beat them in the open, at their own game.

It was the sprinkling of frontiersmen which made this possible, for it was precisely these men in Morgan's ranks who, like their chief, were unimpressed by the reputation of the world's most famous troops.

Their weapons had been proved earlier and commanded respect even from British infantry officers who would remain devoted to the Brown Bess musket throughout their lives. As it had happened at Kings Mountain and elsewhere, the British fired their mass volleys high, and did not kill; American lead worked havoc, especially among the conspicuously-uniformed officers.

At Cowan's Ford, the only premeditated river clash between the armies in the long chase, the British regular acquitted himself well under the worst of conditions. By quirks of circumstance, it was the very slowness of Cornwallis in the early chase that made possible the easy crossing at Cowan's.

If he had come earlier, he would likely have faced the men of Morgan, with both Morgan and Greene on the far bank to direct the defense. If veterans had been behind the rifles at Cowan's, rather than the little band of recently joined militia, there would have been a major action at the Catawba, if the British had crossed at all.

The little action at the ford cost Cornwallis more men—the exact toll is unknown—but was not significant in total casualties. It demonstrated to Americans once more the opposite side of the Cowpens coin: It was not enough for men to be fighting for their homes; they must be hardened and trained, and have leaders in whom they trusted.

In detail, the defense of Cowan's Ford was poorly handled but, except for the death of Davidson, might have become vigorous enough to turn back the British. Greene, and to a lesser extent Morgan, was forced to the choice of whether to remain on this stream or to put Morgan's force on the road for the Yadkin as promptly as possible, and they made the inevitable move. The price of defeat in the rain at Cowan's Ford, though it included the life of Brig. Gen. William Davidson, was small in light of the stakes—the escape of the victors of Cowpens.

The run for the Yadkin was guided, like every step of the campaign from the Catawba to its end, by the keen mind of Greene, who applied himself to his problems with a rare intensity. His subordinates remarked on the Quaker's quick grasp of the situation soon after his arrival in Charlotte and again at the Catawba—and historians afterward took note of his shrewd use of the rivers in his path. His attention to logistics, the hazards of the North Carolina geography, and the supply of men and materials were vital ingredients of victory. There were times when both Morgan and Greene appeared to despair, at least in their letters and dispatches, but there was not a day of bootless, headlong flight. Cornwallis was sometimes forced to do no more than lunge after them in pursuit, but Greene appeared to know his objective clearly in every case—and to the end proved that they were the correct ones.

An army often barefoot, existing on marginal rations, sometimes pressed for powder and shot, was because of Greene's shrewdness enabled to cross the rivers in quick fashion—and to deny such passage to the enemy. This was not entirely because Greene operated in a country which was friendly. The boats built by the Quaker and carried in his wagons might have been matched by an imaginative pursuer; in this event, the campaign would never have reached Guilford Courthouse.

Greene's lieutenants, taking a cue from their commander, seemed also more flexible of mind, and were less bound by the formalities of military tradition than their British counterparts; in this case the casual army was the more effective, more often using the terrain as an ally. In the strict sense no professional soldiers marched with Greene, and as has so often happened throughout history, this proved more of an advantage than a handicap. There were no staff-officer liabilities in Greene's command. He did not inherit these assets, but created an atmosphere for them; in the time of his predecessor, Gates, command relationships were chaotic, largely because of that commander's inability to seize control. A man of rare common sense and initiative, Greene assembled a staff of men of the same stripe.

The campaign, in retrospect, had many turnings: Cowpens damaged the invading force and set off the hapless chase of the Americans; the crossing of the Yadkin made possible Greene's dash toward safety, and when this was offset by the rapid British moves of mid-February, an even more accomplished march was made by Greene to the Dan. The recrossing of the Dan by the Americans was the most fateful move since Greene's division of the army in South Carolina, and even had he not determined to meet Cornwallis in open battle, as he did at Guilford Courthouse, this might have won back North Carolina. The British could not long have withstood the hit-and-run tactics used by Greene, Lee, and Otho Williams in late February and early March.

Guilford Courthouse, as Greene himself realized, was a test of the lessons of the campaign. Though he had waited until he accumulated a superior force, he met the enemy in

much the same spirit, and in almost precisely the same formation, as Morgan had met them at Cowpens. If he, like
Morgan, had rallied his militia screen in the third line, he
would probably have destroyed Cornwallis.

Underlying Greene's decision to fight this battle was
perhaps the single most important development of the winter's
long fighting: An American army had at last come to look
upon the enemy without fear because it was no longer awed
by superior reputation, by allegedly superior arms, training,
tactics, uniforms, and a long tradition of military superiority.

The North Carolina militiamen who ran from the first
line had not achieved that confident state of mind, but the
veterans on their flanks had, and to some degree the Virginians of the second line had, as well. In the case of the third
line, except for the green Second Maryland, and on the far
left American flank where Lee's Legion and Campbell's riflemen fought, the rebels asked no quarter. The quality of their
fighting drew tribute from Cornwallis which expressed something like awe.

It would be almost 170 years before American troops
fought another major war in which such irregular warfare
was possible, but then, in Korea, they would learn some of
this same bitter lesson which was forced upon Cornwallis.
It was another version of the Emperor's Clothes, so persuasively rendered by Daniel Morgan and Nathanael Greene
and their field officers as to strip the renowned British in-
fantryman to the status of an ordinary mortal. When Guilford Courthouse was over, no one in the British camp retained unshaken confidence in the old tradition, the old
discipline, the old formations, the old weapons. Cornwallis
won the ground, but knew very well that he had been out-
fought. It was a new experience for him.

The Carolinas campaign was unique in the Revolution, and fighting in the north, largely because it followed traditional patterns, favored the British almost without exception. The sniping from fence rows in the early skirmishing in Massachusetts was a nursery game by comparison with the bushwhacking by the mountain men in the south. It was only when the British regular met the southern frontiersman in significant numbers that he faltered, and it was Morgan and Greene who convinced the invaders that these men were more than a match for their elite veterans.

The casualties of Guilford Courthouse, added to those of Cowpens, Cowan's Ford, and the constant skirmishes, reduced by about half the potential force of Cornwallis at Yorktown and in a broad sense made possible the combination of circumstances which trapped his Lordship between the French fleet and the armies of Washington and Rochambeau. The tactics which caused these casualties were of the frontier, the hit-and-run raid, the ambush and fighting retreat which in similar forms had been used by partisan and guerrilla forces for centuries. Nathanael Greene may have found inspiration for his campaign strategy in one of the classic texts on war which so fascinated him, by Saxe or Turenne or some other, but the day-by-day fighting to which his cavalry and his light infantry were so ideally suited was unknown to West European warfare. In the form used by Morgan and the backwoodsmen, this kind of war was a product of the American frontier; since the frontier no longer lay on the Eastern Seaboard in the north, the Revolution had to sweep south to meet it. There was Indian fighting in the west, but there was nothing to match this campaign of Greene and Cornwallis.

There had been just four months and three days between Greene's assumption of command of his shadow army in Charlotte on Dec. 3 and his taking the road to the conquest of South Carolina on Apr. 6. Almost exactly half of this time had elapsed between Cowpens and Guilford Courthouse, during which the Quaker conducted one of the most remarkable retreats in military history. When he began, the cause seemed to be hopeless; when he had done, the foundation for final victory had been laid, and the end was only six months away.

When Greene had been sent south, to create his own army, his own plans, and his own system of supply, George Washington had not fought a major battle in three years. Since Monmouth, the large armies of the north had not clashed, yet Washington could find no troops to aid Greene. The attention of America and Great Britain remained fixed on the north even as Greene and Morgan doggedly produced their miracles against the most famous British soldier in the field. The public gaze remained riveted in its accustomed place, on the army of George Washington, and only late in 1781, with astonishment, turned south to note the end of the drama at Yorktown.

In the year of its winning, as in the generations afterward, Greene's campaign in the south went largely unnoticed and unsung, for all of its spectacular figures, chilling hardships, and contribution to American victory. The personality of Quaker Greene may have been responsible. Daniel Morgan at Cowpens caught the eye, and Light-Horse Harry Lee, and Francis Marion—but not Greene, though he might be styled the most able field commander in the American armies. Not only was Greene modest, and far from flamboyant, but despite his inexorable will to build an efficient army, war was not his love, and he was moved to pity when, late in the campaign, he saw the devastation in South Carolina, and wrote his wife:

> . . . I wish I was there with you, free from the bustle of the world and the miseries of war. My nature recoils at the horrid scenes which this country affords, and longs for a peaceful retirement where love and softer pleasures are to be found. Here, turn what way you will, you have nothing but the mournful widow and the plaints of the fatherless child; and behold nothing but houses desolated and plantations laid waste. Ruin is in every form and misery in every shape.

Yet Greene resisted everyone who opposed the strengthening of his southern army, even George Washington. When the Commander in Chief took for his own some troops bound for Greene's headquarters a few days before Cornwallis surrendered at Yorktown, Greene wrote him:

> I am informed that the Maryland troops, who were expected to reinforce this army, have been ordered to join the army in Virginia. Our situation is truly distressing, and the want of a reinforcement very pressing; but if it will interfere with more important concerns, I am willing to struggle with every difficulty and inconvenience.

Harry Lee was more outspoken in his criticism of the loss of these troops and the concentration at Yorktown: "No troops coming on to you, but a perfect monopoly has taken place of men and supplies, to fight a deranged, small army." The same "deranged, small army" Lee and Greene had fought for so long, and had so willingly helped on its way.

ACKNOWLEDGMENTS

I am indebted to Dr. H. Frank Rankin, of Tulane University, a veteran student of the Campaign of 1781 in the Carolinas. His unpublished master's thesis on the subject was of value to me, and his guidance invaluable. This narrative is based largely on a study made by the writer in 1950, which produced the novel *The Ragged Ones*. Except for the work of Rankin, little new material has since appeared. The bibliography which follows was used extensively.

Of special value were the Orderly Book of the British army for this period, the narratives of soldiers like Henry Lee, Banastre Tarleton, Charles Cornwallis, Henry Clinton—and of the lesser figures in the ranks like Enoch Anderson, James Collins, Robert Henry and Roger Lamb.

The historian Stedman, who rode with Cornwallis, provided one point of view, but this was frequently at odds with the testimony of Lamb, Cornwallis, Tarleton and others with the invading force—and all, of course, differed from the accounts left by Lee and other Americans.

Biographies of Greene which were used most frequently were those of William Johnson and George Washington Greene. Recent lives of Daniel Morgan by North Callahan and Donald Higginbotham were also used.

Among works of local historians not listed in the bibliography, I depended upon Judge David Schenck's sound and venerable *North Carolina, 1781,* and upon the Reverend Eli Caruthers's *Interesting Revolutionary Incidents.*

Since I have lived for ten years in the old Hoskins farmhouse cabin, used by the British as hospital and headquarters, I have also collected incidental lore on the battle in the Guilford neighborhood.

I must also extend my thanks to Eugene D. McKeown, superintendent, and Robert S. McDaniel, historian, of the Guilford Courthouse National Military Park, and to Charles R. Sanders, Jr., of Raleigh, North Carolina.

BURKE DAVIS

Cornwallis House
Greensboro, North Carolina

Bibliography

Anderson, Enoch, *Personal Recollections* (Wilmington, Del., 1896).

Balch, Thomas (ed.), *Papers Relating Chiefly to the Maryland Line during the Revolution* (Philadelphia, 1857).

Bass, Robert D., *The Green Dragoon* (New York, 1957).

Blackmore, Howard A., *British Military Firearms* (London, 1961).

Boyd, Julian, *The Papers of Thomas Jefferson* (12 vols. to date; Princeton, N.J., 1950–61).

Callahan, North, *Daniel Morgan, Ranger of the Revolution* (New York, 1960).

Clinton, Sir Henry, *Narrative of the Campaign in 1781 in North America* (Philadelphia, 1865).

——, *Observations on Earl Cornwallis' Answer* (Philadelphia, 1866).

Collins, James P., *Autobiography of a Revolutionary Soldier* (John M. Roberts, ed.; Clinton, La., 1859).

Cornwallis, Charles, *Answer to Sir Henry Clinton's Narrative of the Campaign in 1781 in North America* (Philadelphia, 1866).

——, *Correspondence of Charles, First Marquis Cornwallis* (Charles Ross, ed.; 3 vols.; London, 1859).

Dawson, H. B., *Battles of the United States by Sea and Land* (2 vols.; New York, 1858).

Eelking, Max von, *The German Allied Troops in the North American War of Independence* (J. G. Rosengarten, trans.; Albany, N.Y., 1893).

Force, Peter (ed.), *American Archives* (9 vols.; Washington, 1837-53).

Gibbes, Robert W., *Documentary History of the American Revolution* (3 vols.; New York, 1853-57).

Graham, James, *The Life of General Daniel Morgan* (New York, 1856).

Graham, William A., *General Joseph Graham and His Papers on North Carolina Revolutionary History* (Raleigh, N.C., 1904).

Greene, George W., *The Life of Nathanael Greene* (3 vols.; New York, 1867-71).

Henry, Robert, *Narrative of the Battle of Cowan's Ford* . . . (Greensboro, N.C., 1891).

Higginbotham, Donald, *Daniel Morgan, Revolutionary Rifleman* (Williamsburg, Va., 1961).

Jarrell, Mary, *Olde Guilford Almanac*, 1958-61 (Annual, Greensboro, N. C.)

Johnson, William, *Sketches of the Life and Correspondence of Nathanael Greene* (2 vols.; Charleston, S.C., 1822).

Lamb, Roger, *An Original and Authentic Journal of Occurrences during the Late American War* (Dublin, 1809).

Lazenby, Mary Elinor, *The Catawba Frontier* (Washington, 1950).

Lee, Henry, *The Campaign of 1781 in the Carolinas* (Philadelphia, 1824).

——, *Memoirs of the War in the Southern Department of the United States* (Robert E. Lee, ed.; New York, 1870).

Lossing, Benjamin J., *The Pictorial Field-book of the Revolution* (2 vols.; New York, 1859).

Mackenzie, Roderick, *Strictures on Lt.-Col. Tarleton's "History of the Campaigns of 1780 and 1781"* (London, 1787).

Moore, Frank (ed.), *Diary of the American Revolution* (2 vols.; New York, 1860).

Muller, John, *Treatise on Artillery* (Philadelphia, 1779).

Newsome, A. R., "A British Orderly Book, 1780-1781" (*North Carolina Historical Review*, Jan.-Oct., 1932).

Peterson, Harold L., "The Brown Bess" (*Military Collector and Historian*, Dec., 1951).

Rankin, Hugh F., *Greene and Cornwallis: The Campaign in the Carolinas, 1780-1781* (unpublished Master's thesis, University of North Carolina).

Robinson, Blackwell, *William R. Davie* (Chapel Hill, N.C., 1957).

Seymour, William, *A Journal of the Southern Expedition, 1780–1783* (Wilmington, Del., 1896).

Sparks, Jared (ed.), *Correspondence of the American Revolution* (4 vols.; Boston, 1853).

Stedman, Charles, *The History of . . . the American War* (2 vols.; London, 1794).

Tarleton, Lt. Col. Banastre, *A History of the Campaigns of 1780 and 1781* (Dublin, 1787).

Tiffany, Osmond, *A Sketch of the Life and Services of Gen. Otho Holland Williams* (Baltimore, 1851).

Tucker, St. George, "The Southern Campaign, 1781 . . . in the Letters from Judge Tucker to his Wife" (Charles W. Coleman, ed.; *The Magazine of American History*, VII [1881]).

Young, Thomas, "Memoir of . . . a Revolutionary Patriot of South Carolina" (*The Orion*, III [Oct., 1843]).

INDEX